# THE
# TOP 100
# QUICK & EASY
# SAUCES

THE
# TOP 100
# QUICK & EASY
# SAUCES

**MOUTH-WATERING CLASSIC AND CONTEMPORARY RECIPES**

DUNCAN BAIRD PUBLISHERS

LONDON

**The Top 100 Quick & Easy Sauces**
Anne Sheasby

First published in the United Kingdom and Ireland in 2010 by
Duncan Baird Publishers Ltd
Sixth Floor, Castle House
75–76 Wells Street
London W1T 3QH

Conceived, created and designed by Duncan Baird Publishers

Copyright © Duncan Baird Publishers 2005, 2010
Text copyright © Anne Sheasby 2005, 2010
Photography copyright © Duncan Baird Publishers 2005,
2010

The right of Anne Sheasby to be identified as the Author of
this text has been asserted in accordance with the Copyright,
Designs and Patents Act of 1988.

Managing Editor: Grace Cheetham
Editor: Alison Bolus
Managing Designer: Manisha Patel
Designer: Luana Gobbo
Commissioned photography: William Lingwood, Simon Smith
and Toby Scott
Food Stylist: Lucy McKelvie
Prop Stylist: Helen Trent

British Library Cataloguing-in-Publication Data:
A CIP record for this book is available from the British Library

ISBN: 978-1-84483-896-7

10 9 8 7 6 5 4 3 2 1

Typeset in News Gothic
Colour reproduction by Colourscan, Singapore
Printed in Malaysia for Imago

**Publisher's Note**
While every care has been taken in compiling the recipes for
this book, Duncan Baird Publishers, or any other persons
who have been involved in working on this publication,
cannot accept responsibility for any errors or omissions,
inadvertent or not, that may be found in the recipes or text,
nor for any problems that may arise as a result of preparing
one of these recipes. If you are pregnant or breastfeeding or
have any special dietary requirements or medical conditions,
it is advisable to consult a medical professional before
following any of the recipes contained in this book.

**Notes on the Recipes**
Unless otherwise stated:
Use medium eggs, fruit and vegetables
Use fresh ingredients, including herbs
Do not mix metric and imperial measurements
1 tsp = 5ml   1 tbsp = 15ml   1 cup = 250ml
• Some of the recipes in this book contain raw or lightly
cooked eggs – these recipes are not recommended for babies
and young children, pregnant women, the elderly and those
convalescing.

# CONTENTS

# SAUCE BASICS

A good sauce can provide the finishing touch to many dishes, complementing and enhancing the flavour of the most simple food without being overpowering. A grilled steak, chicken portion or fish cutlet can be transformed into something really special with the addition of a good sauce. Sauces not only add flavour and colour to dishes, they also add texture and moisture, and there is a whole variety to suit all tastes and palates – savoury and sweet, rich and light, hot and cold.

## TYPES OF SAUCES

There are several types of sauce, including roux-based, brown or emulsified sauces, vegetable-based sauces and purées, gravies and flavoured butters, as well as salsas, relishes, salad dressings and vinaigrettes and savoury and sweet dips, plus sweet sauces, fruit pureés and coulis.

### ROUX-BASED SAUCES

A roux is a blend of equal quantities of melted butter and plain flour that are cooked together before liquid, such as milk or stock, is gradually stirred or whisked into it over a gentle heat to make a béchamel sauce. Once the sauce has come to the boil and thickened, it is left to simmer gently for 2–3 minutes to cook out the taste of the flour.

With a classic White or Béchamel Sauce, the roux is cooked but not coloured, whereas for brown sauces, such as Espagnole (Brown) Sauce, the roux is cooked until it becomes brown.

### EMULSIFIED SAUCES

Emulsified sauces are based on one of two emulsions – a butter emulsion (such as Hollandaise Sauce or Beurre Blanc) or a cold emulsion of oil and egg yolks such as Mayonnaise. With a butter emulsion, the initial cooking liquid used for the sauce is reduced during cooking to give a more intense flavour to the sauce, which is then enriched and thickened with butter or eggs.

## FRUIT PUREES AND COULIS

These are simple to make and create a delicious fruit sauce to accompany desserts such as fresh fruit, ice cream or meringues, as well as adding a lovely visual finishing touch.

Fruit coulis are made by first puréeing raw or lightly cooked fruit. The purée is then sieved, sweetened and sometimes flavoured with liqueur, to give a delicious and colourful pouring sauce.

Fruits such as raspberries, strawberries, mixed berries, mangoes, peaches and apricots are ideal for making fruit coulis. Some fruit- or vegetable-based sauces can also be thickened by blending the ingredients together using a hand-held blender, or a small blender or food processor.

## THICKENING SAUCES

Sauces may be thickened in various ways at different stages of a recipe. Sometimes a sauce is thickened at the beginning of a recipe with a roux, or towards the end of a recipe using egg yolks, butter or cream. Another thickener that is added towards the end of the preparation time is beurre manié – equal quantities of softened butter and plain flour kneaded together to make a smooth paste, which is then gradually whisked into the hot cooked sauce or liquid until it thickens.

Sauces may also be thickened using cornflour, arrowroot or potato flour blended with a little cold milk or water, then added to the sauce and heated, while stirring, until the sauce comes to the boil and thickens. Serve sauces thickened with arrowroot or potato flour as soon as they have thickened – if they are allowed to simmer for more than 1 minute or so, they may become thin again. Sauces thickened with cornflour need to be simmered gently for 2–3 minutes.

## REDUCING SAUCES

An alternative method of thickening sauces is to boil the mixture rapidly until it has reduced in volume. Do not season the sauce until it is reduced, as reducing will intensify the flavours. Once the sauce is reduced, skim off any froth from the surface using a slotted or metal spoon. Do not attempt to reduce a sauce containing eggs or yogurt by this method as it is likely to curdle. Quick cream sauces can usually be reduced in this way, but those using crème fraîche may curdle.

# Chapter 1

# BASIC & CLASSIC SAUCES

Basic sauces are an important element of everyday cooking. This chapter brings together a wide selection of good, basic sauces, such as Basic White Sauce, Rich Cheese Sauce and Béarnaise Sauce, which can be served simply, perhaps with meat, fish or vegetables. Other essential sauces, such as Rich Tomato Sauce, which can be used as the basis for tempting recipes such as meat or vegetable lasagnes, are also covered.

Many of the classic sauces, such as Mayonnaise, Aïoli and Hollandaise, will be familiar to you, though perhaps you have not tried to make them before, while others, such as Velouté Sauce, Bordelaise Sauce and Saffron Sauce, may be less familiar. Once you have mastered a few easy basic techniques, you can enjoy creating a whole range of classic sauces at home, and you will never want to go back to ready-made products again.

Herby Lemon Hollandaise (see page 27)

# 001 Basic White Sauce (Pouring Sauce)

**PREPARATION TIME** 5 minutes   **COOKING TIME** 10 minutes   **SERVES** 4

15g/½oz butter
1 tbsp plain flour

300ml/10fl oz/1¼ cups milk
salt and freshly ground black pepper

1 Melt the butter in a small saucepan, stir in the flour and cook, stirring, for 1 minute. Remove the pan from the heat and gradually stir or whisk in the milk.

2 Return the pan to the heat and bring slowly to the boil, stirring or whisking until the sauce is thickened and smooth. Simmer gently for 2–3 minutes, stirring continuously. Season to taste with salt and pepper. Serve hot.

**SERVING SUGGESTIONS** Serve with grilled gammon steaks or chicken breasts. Alternatively, serve with grilled fillets of plaice or sole, or with cooked broad beans or green beans.

# 002 Creamy White Wine Sauce

**PREPARATION TIME** 10 minutes   **COOKING TIME** 20 minutes   **SERVES** 4–6

175ml/6fl oz/⅔ cup dry white wine
200ml/7fl oz/¾ cup double cream
100ml/3½fl oz/⅓ cup fish or vegetable
   stock (homemade or from a stock cube)

1 tbsp chopped dill or chervil (optional)
1 tbsp chopped parsley
salt and freshly ground black pepper

1 Pour the wine into a saucepan, bring to the boil and boil rapidly until reduced by half.
2 Stir in the cream and stock and bring back to the boil, then reduce the heat and simmer, uncovered, for 10–15 minutes, or until the sauce thickens slightly, stirring occasionally.
3 Remove the pan from the heat and stir in the dill, if using, and parsley. Season to taste with salt and pepper. Serve hot.

**SERVING SUGGESTIONS** Serve with grilled, baked or pan-fried whole plaice or lemon sole.

# 003 Rich Cheese Sauce

**PREPARATION TIME** 10 minutes   **COOKING TIME** 10 minutes   **SERVES** 4

15g/½oz butter

1 tbsp plain flour

300ml/10fl oz/1¼ cups full-fat milk

85g/3oz mature Cheddar cheese, grated

2 tbsp freshly grated Parmesan cheese

1 tsp Dijon mustard

freshly grated nutmeg, to taste (optional)

salt and freshly ground black pepper

1 Melt the butter in a small saucepan, stir in the flour and cook, stirring, for 1 minute. Remove the pan from the heat and gradually stir or whisk in the milk.

2 Return the pan to the heat and bring slowly to the boil, stirring or whisking until the sauce is thickened and smooth.

3 Stir in the cheeses and mustard and cook over a gentle heat for about 5 minutes, or until the cheeses have melted and the sauce is smooth and glossy, stirring continuously. Season to taste with salt and pepper, and a little nutmeg, if using. Serve hot.

**SERVING SUGGESTIONS** Serve with oven-baked gammon or ham, or with grilled cod or halibut. Alternatively, serve with cooked cauliflower or broccoli florets, or with hot gnocchi or macaroni.
**VARIATIONS** Use red Leicester or double Gloucester cheese in place of Cheddar and Parmesan. Use English mustard in place of Dijon mustard.

# 004 **Béarnaise Sauce**

**PREPARATION TIME** 10 minutes   **COOKING TIME** 15 minutes   **SERVES** 4–6

3 tbsp tarragon or white wine vinegar

½ tsp black peppercorns

2 shallots, finely chopped

a few tarragon sprigs

1 bay leaf

2 egg yolks

115g/4oz butter, at room temperature, diced

1–2 tbsp chopped mixed herbs, such as
tarragon, parsley and chervil

freshly squeezed lemon juice, to taste
(optional)

salt and freshly ground black pepper

1 Put the vinegar in a small saucepan with the peppercorns, shallots, tarragon sprigs, bay leaf
and 1 tbsp water. Bring to the boil, then simmer until the mixture has reduced to about 1 tbsp
of liquid. Remove the pan from the heat and set aside.

2 Put the egg yolks in a heatproof bowl with 15g/½oz of the butter and a pinch of salt
and beat together using a balloon whisk. Strain the reduced vinegar into the egg mixture and
stir to mix.

3 Put the bowl over a pan of barely simmering water and whisk the egg mixture for about
4 minutes, or until pale and beginning to thicken.

4 Gradually whisk in the remaining butter, one piece at a time, until the mixture begins to thicken
and emulsify. Make sure each piece of butter is incorporated into the sauce before adding the
next piece.

5 Once all the butter has been added and the sauce has become light and thick, remove the bowl
from the heat. Whisk for 1 minute. Stir in the herbs and season with salt and pepper to taste.
Add a small squeeze of lemon juice, if desired. Serve immediately.

**SERVING SUGGESTIONS** Serve with grilled cod or salmon steaks. Alternatively, serve with grilled or pan-
fried beef or lamb steaks, or with steamed asparagus, green beans or baby courgettes.

# 005 Velouté Sauce

**PREPARATION TIME** 5 minutes   **COOKING TIME** 10 minutes   **SERVES** 4–6

20g/¾oz butter
3 tbsp plain flour
300ml/10fl oz/1¼ cups chicken, fish,
   vegetable or meat stock (homemade or
   from a stock cube)

2 tbsp double cream
½ tsp freshly squeezed lemon juice
salt and freshly ground black pepper

1 Melt the butter in a small saucepan, stir in the flour and cook, stirring, for about 2 minutes, or
   until light golden in colour. Remove the pan from the heat and gradually stir or whisk in the stock.
2 Return the pan to the heat and bring slowly to the boil, stirring or whisking until the sauce is
   thickened and smooth. Simmer gently for 2–3 minutes, stirring continuously.
3 Stir in the cream, then stir in the lemon juice. Season to taste with salt and pepper. Serve hot.

**SERVING SUGGESTIONS** Serve with grilled or baked chicken breasts, or fillets of cod or plaice. Alternatively,
serve with grilled lamb or pork chops.

# 006 Rich Tomato Sauce

PREPARATION TIME 5 minutes   COOKING TIME 45 minutes   SERVES 4–6

40g/1½oz butter
1 red onion, finely chopped
2 garlic cloves, crushed
800g/1lb 12oz/3⅓ cups tinned
   chopped tomatoes

150ml/5fl oz/⅔ cup red wine
2 tbsp tomato purée
½ tsp granulated sugar
1 bouquet garni
salt and freshly ground black pepper

1 Melt the butter in a saucepan, add the onion and garlic and sauté gently for about 10 minutes, or until softened.
2 Add the tomatoes, wine, tomato purée, sugar and bouquet garni and mix well. Bring to the boil, then reduce the heat and cook gently, uncovered, for about 30 minutes, or until the sauce is thick and pulpy, stirring occasionally.
3 Discard the bouquet garni and season to taste with salt and pepper. Serve hot.

SERVING SUGGESTIONS Serve with hot pasta such as tagliatelle or fusilli, or use as the basis for a vegetable or meat lasagne. Alternatively, serve with meatballs or cooked vegetables.

# 007 **Barbecue Sauce**

**PREPARATION TIME** 10 minutes   **COOKING TIME** 20 minutes   **SERVES** 4–6

25g/1oz butter

1 red onion, finely chopped

400g/14oz/scant 1⅔ cups tinned chopped
   tomatoes

4 tbsp light beer or lager
   (such as Budweiser)

1 tbsp red wine vinegar

1 tbsp Worcestershire sauce

1 tbsp tomato purée

1 tbsp light soft brown sugar

2 tsp Dijon mustard

salt and freshly ground black pepper

1 Melt the butter in a saucepan, add the onion and sauté for about 5 minutes, or until softened.

2 Add the tomatoes, beer, vinegar, Worcestershire sauce, tomato purée, sugar and mustard and
   stir to mix well.

3 Bring slowly to the boil, stirring, then simmer, uncovered, for 10–15 minutes, or until the sauce
   thickens slightly, stirring occasionally. Season to taste with salt and pepper. Serve hot.

**SERVING SUGGESTIONS** Serve with barbecued vegetable or chicken kebabs, or chicken drumsticks.

# 008 Soubise (Onion) Sauce

**PREPARATION TIME** 10 minutes   **COOKING TIME** 20 minutes   **SERVES** 4

40g/1½oz butter
1 large onion, finely chopped
2 tbsp plain flour

300ml/10fl oz/1¼ cups milk
salt and freshly ground black pepper

1 Melt half of the butter in a saucepan, add the onion and sauté gently for 10–15 minutes, or
   until softened. Remove the pan from the heat and set aside.
2 Melt the remaining butter in a separate saucepan, stir in the flour and cook, stirring, for
   1 minute. Remove the pan from the heat and gradually stir or whisk in the milk.
3 Return the pan to the heat and bring slowly to the boil, stirring or whisking until the sauce is
   thickened and smooth. Simmer gently for 2–3 minutes, stirring continuously.
4 Stir in the sautéed onion and reheat gently until hot, stirring continuously. Season to taste with
   salt and pepper. Serve hot.

**SERVING SUGGESTIONS** Serve with baked gammon or roast chicken, or with grilled haddock or monkfish.
**VARIATION** Use 1 large red onion in place of the standard onion.
**COOK'S TIP** Leave the root end intact when slicing or chopping an onion. This will prevent the release of the
strong juices and fumes that cause eyes to water.

# 009 Creamy Mushroom Sauce

**PREPARATION TIME** 10 minutes   **COOKING TIME** 15 minutes   **SERVES** 4–6

150ml/5fl oz/⅔ cup vegetable stock
   (homemade or from a stock cube)
300ml/10fl oz/1¼ cups double cream
40g/1½oz butter
175g/6oz/3 cups chestnut or brown-cap
   mushrooms, sliced

115g/4oz/2 cups button mushrooms, sliced
1–2 tbsp chopped mixed herbs, such as
   parsley, chives and marjoram or oregano
salt and freshly ground black pepper

1 Pour the stock and cream into a saucepan. Bring slowly to the boil, then simmer gently until
   the sauce thickens slightly, enough to coat the back of a wooden spoon, stirring frequently.
2 Meanwhile, melt the butter in a frying pan, add all the mushrooms and sauté for about
   5 minutes, or until softened. Increase the heat slightly and cook, stirring frequently, until all the
   liquid has evaporated.
3 Add the mushrooms and chopped herbs to the cream sauce and reheat gently until hot, stirring
   continuously. Season to taste with salt and pepper. Serve hot.

**SERVING SUGGESTIONS** Serve with grilled chicken breasts or barbecued beef steaks. Alternatively, serve
with baked cod or haddock fillets, or tuna steaks.
**VARIATIONS** Use crème fraîche in place of double cream. Use mixed wild mushrooms
in place of chestnut or button mushrooms.

# 010 Bordelaise Sauce

**PREPARATION TIME** 10 minutes   **COOKING TIME** 1 hour 15 minutes   **SERVES** 4–6

25g/1oz butter
1 rindless unsmoked back bacon rasher,
   finely chopped
2 shallots, finely chopped
1 carrot, finely chopped
55g/2oz/1 cup mushrooms, finely chopped

3 tbsp plain flour
300ml/10fl oz/1¼ cups beef stock
   (homemade or from a stock cube)
300ml/10fl oz/1¼ cups red wine
1 bouquet garni
salt and freshly ground black pepper

1 Melt the butter in a saucepan. Add the bacon and cook for 2 minutes, stirring. Add the shallots, carrot and mushrooms and sauté for about 8 minutes, or until softened and lightly browned.

2 Stir in the flour and cook, stirring, until the flour is lightly browned. Remove the pan from the heat and gradually stir or whisk in the stock and wine. Return the pan to the heat and bring slowly to the boil, stirring continuously, and cook until the mixture thickens. Add the bouquet garni and salt and pepper to taste. Cover and simmer gently for 1 hour, stirring occasionally.

3 Remove the pan from the heat, let cool slightly, then strain the sauce through a sieve. Discard the contents of the sieve. Return the strained sauce to the rinsed-out saucepan and reheat gently before serving. Adjust the seasoning to taste. Serve hot.

**SERVING SUGGESTIONS** Serve with pan-fried beef medallions, or with roast lamb, pheasant or rabbit.
**VARIATION** Use smoked bacon in place of unsmoked bacon.

# 011 Parsley Sauce

PREPARATION TIME 5 minutes   COOKING TIME 10 minutes   SERVES 4

15g/½oz butter
1 tbsp plain flour
300ml/10fl oz/1¼ cups milk

2–3 tbsp chopped parsley
salt and freshly ground black pepper

1 Melt the butter in a small saucepan, stir in the flour and cook, stirring, for 1 minute. Remove the pan from the heat and gradually stir or whisk in the milk.

2 Return the pan to the heat and bring slowly to the boil, stirring or whisking until the sauce is thickened and smooth. Simmer gently for 2–3 minutes, stirring continuously.

3 Stir in the parsley and season to taste with salt and pepper. Serve hot.

**SERVING SUGGESTIONS** Serve with grilled fillets of cod or haddock. Alternatively, serve with baked glazed ham, or with cooked broad beans, baby sweetcorn or spinach.
**VARIATIONS** Use 150ml/5fl oz/⅔ cup vegetable stock or double cream in place of 150ml/5fl oz/⅔ cup of the milk. Use 1–2 tbsp chopped mixed herbs in place of parsley.
**COOK'S TIP** For a thicker Parsley Sauce, simply follow the recipe above but increase the quantities of butter to 25g/1oz and flour to 4½ tsp.

# 012 Saffron Sauce

**PREPARATION TIME** 20 minutes plus soaking   **COOKING TIME** 20 minutes   **SERVES** 4

½ tsp saffron strands
40g/1½oz chilled butter, diced
2 shallots, finely chopped
4 tbsp dry white wine

1 recipe quantity Velouté Sauce
  (see page 14)
salt and freshly ground black pepper

1 Crumble the saffron strands into a small bowl, add 2 tbsp hot water and leave to soak for
   15 minutes.
2 Melt 15g/½oz of the butter in a saucepan, add the shallots and sauté for 5 minutes, or until
   softened. Add the wine and let bubble gently until the liquid has reduced to about 1 tbsp.
3 Add the saffron and the soaking liquid to the pan and whisk in the Velouté Sauce. Heat gently
   until boiling, stirring, then simmer gently for 10 minutes, stirring occasionally.
4 Remove the pan from the heat and season to taste with salt and pepper. Gradually whisk in the
   remaining butter until well blended. Serve hot.

**SERVING SUGGESTIONS** Serve with grilled or poached haddock fillets or monkfish tail.

# 013 Quick Chilli Sauce

**PREPARATION TIME** 10 minutes   **COOKING TIME** 20 minutes   **SERVES** 6

1 tbsp olive oil or chilli-flavoured olive oil

5 spring onions, finely chopped

1 red chilli, deseeded and finely chopped

1 garlic clove, crushed

400g/14oz/scant 1⅔ cups tinned chopped
   tomatoes

a squeeze of fresh lemon juice

1 tbsp light soft brown sugar

2 tsp cornflour

bottled medium-hot chilli sauce,
   to taste (optional)

salt and freshly ground black pepper

1 Heat the oil in a small saucepan, add the spring onions, chilli and garlic and sauté for about
   5 minutes, or until softened.

2 Add the tomatoes, lemon juice, sugar, and salt and pepper to taste, and mix well. Bring slowly
   to the boil, then cover and simmer gently for 10 minutes, stirring occasionally.

3 Put the cornflour and 1 tbsp cold water in a small bowl and blend until smooth, then stir the
   cornflour mixture into the sauce. Bring the sauce to the boil, stirring continuously, then reduce
   the heat and simmer gently for 3 minutes, stirring.

4 Taste, and add more salt and pepper if desired, and add a dash or two of bottled chilli sauce, if
   using. Serve hot.

**SERVING SUGGESTIONS** Serve with grilled or pan-fried monkfish, halibut or prawns. Alternatively, serve
with stuffed baked courgettes, marrows or peppers.

# 014 **Red Wine Sauce**

**PREPARATION TIME** 10 minutes   **COOKING TIME** 15 minutes   **SERVES** 4–6

25g/1oz butter

2–3 shallots, finely chopped

1 small garlic clove, crushed

2 tbsp plain flour

2 tsp light soft brown sugar

300ml/10fl oz/1¼ cups burgundy
 or red wine

1 tbsp medium-dry sherry

1 tsp chopped thyme or rosemary

salt and freshly ground black pepper

1 Melt the butter in a small saucepan, add the shallots and garlic and sauté gently for about
   10 minutes, or until softened.

2 Stir in the flour and sugar and cook for 1 minute, stirring. Remove the pan from the heat and
   gradually stir or whisk in the wine and sherry.

3 Return the pan to the heat and bring slowly to the boil, stirring or whisking continuously until
   the sauce is thickened. Simmer gently for 2–3 minutes, stirring.

4 Stir in the thyme and season to taste with salt and pepper. Serve hot.

**SERVING SUGGESTIONS** Serve with roast beef, or with grilled lamb or pork chops.
**COOK'S TIP** Choose a red wine with a fairly robust flavour. Once the sauce has been cooked, cool slightly,
then purée in a blender or food processor until smooth, if desired. Reheat gently before serving.

# 015 Mayonnaise

**PREPARATION TIME** 10 minutes   **SERVES** 6–8

2 egg yolks
1 tsp Dijon mustard
1 tbsp freshly squeezed lemon juice or white
   wine vinegar

pinch of caster sugar
375ml/13fl oz/1½ cups light olive oil or
   sunflower oil
salt and freshly ground black pepper

**1** Put the egg yolks, mustard, lemon juice, sugar, a little salt and pepper, and 1 tbsp of the oil in a small blender or food processor. Blend for about 20 seconds, or until smooth, pale and creamy.

**2** With the motor running and the blades turning, gradually add the remaining oil to the blender or food processor, pouring it through the feeder tube in a slow, continuous stream until the mayonnaise is thick, creamy and smooth.

**3** Adjust the seasoning to taste, then use immediately or cover and chill until required. Store in a covered container in the refrigerator for up to 3 days. Remove the mayonnaise from the refrigerator 30 minutes before serving. Serve cold.

**SERVING SUGGESTIONS** Serve with salads, sliced cold meats or smoked fish, or use as the basis for sauces such as Tartare Sauce or flavoured mayonnaises.
**VARIATION** Use fresh lime juice in place of lemon juice or white wine vinegar.
**COOK'S TIP** The ingredients for mayonnaise should all be at room temperature. If eggs are used straight from the refrigerator, the mayonnaise may curdle.

# 016 Aïoli

**PREPARATION TIME** 10 minutes   **SERVES** 6–8

2 egg yolks
1 tbsp freshly squeezed lemon juice
4 garlic cloves, crushed
½ tsp salt

300ml/10fl oz/1¼ cups light olive oil or
   sunflower oil
freshly ground black pepper

1 Put the egg yolks, lemon juice, garlic, salt, a little black pepper and 1 tbsp of the oil in a small
   blender or food processor. Blend for about 20 seconds, or until pale and creamy.

2 With the motor running and the blades turning, gradually add the remaining oil to the blender
   or food processor, pouring it through the feeder tube in a slow, continuous stream until the aïoli
   is thick, creamy and smooth.

3 Adjust the seasoning to taste, then use immediately or cover and chill until required. Store in a
   covered container in the refrigerator for up to 2 days. Serve cold or leave at room temperature
   for 30 minutes before serving.

**SERVING SUGGESTIONS** Serve with sliced cold roast chicken or salmon fillets, tiger prawns, or with
Mediterranean fish soups. Alternatively, serve with hard-boiled eggs or as a dip for potato wedges, crisps or
vegetable crudités.
**VARIATIONS** Use fresh lime juice in place of lemon juice. Use smoked garlic in place of standard garlic.
**COOK'S TIPS** When buying garlic, choose plump garlic bulbs with tightly packed cloves and dry skin. Avoid
bulbs with soft, shrivelled cloves or green shoots.
   When using a garlic press, leave the peel on the garlic clove. The soft garlic flesh will be pressed through
the mesh, and the peel/skin will be left behind in the garlic press, making it easy to clean out after use.

# 017 Herby Lemon Hollandaise

**PREPARATION TIME** 20 minutes   **COOKING TIME** 2–3 minutes   **SERVES** 4–6

3 tbsp white wine vinegar

6 black peppercorns

1 slice of onion or ½ shallot

1 bay leaf

1 blade of mace

2 egg yolks

115g/4oz butter, at room temperature, diced

1 tbsp chopped mixed herbs

freshly squeezed lemon juice, to taste

salt and freshly ground black pepper

1 Put the vinegar in a heavy-based saucepan with the peppercorns, onion, bay leaf and mace. Bring to the boil, then reduce the heat and simmer until the mixture has reduced to about 1 tbsp liquid. Remove from the heat. Set aside.

2 Put the egg yolks in a heatproof bowl with 15g/½oz of the butter and a pinch of salt and beat together using a balloon whisk. Strain the reduced vinegar into the egg mixture and stir to mix.

3 Put the bowl over a pan of barely simmering water and whisk for 3–4 minutes, or until the mixture is pale and beginning to thicken.

4 Gradually whisk in the remaining butter, one piece at a time, until the mixture begins to thicken and emulsify. Make sure each piece of butter is incorporated before adding the next piece.

5 Once all the butter has been added and the sauce has become light and thick, remove the bowl from the heat. Whisk for 1 minute. Stir in the herbs, then adjust the seasoning and add a little lemon juice to taste. Serve immediately.

**SERVING SUGGESTIONS** Serve with salmon fillets or whole rainbow trout.

# 018 Tartare Sauce

**PREPARATION TIME** 10 minutes, plus standing  **SERVES** 8–10

55g/2oz/4 tbsp drained and finely chopped
  gherkins

2 tbsp drained and finely chopped capers

250ml/9fl oz/1 cup Mayonnaise
  (see page 25)

4 tbsp extra-thick double cream

1 tbsp tarragon vinegar

1 tbsp chopped flat-leaf parsley

1 tbsp snipped chives

2 tsp chopped tarragon

salt and freshly ground black pepper

1 Put the gherkins, capers, and mayonnaise in a bowl and mix well, then fold in the cream.

2 Fold in the vinegar and herbs and season to taste with salt and pepper.

3 Cover and leave in a cool place for about 30 minutes before serving, to allow the flavours to
develop. Serve cold.

**SERVING SUGGESTIONS** Serve with grilled or baked fishcakes or fish goujons. Alternatively, serve with fried
breadcrumbed or battered cod, plaice or haddock.

**VARIATIONS** Use plain fromage frais or crème fraîche in place of cream. Use white wine vinegar or freshly
squeezed lemon juice in place of tarragon vinegar.

**COOK'S TIP** Capers are the small, unopened buds of a thorny, wild Mediterranean plant, which are picked
and then pickled in salty vinegar or preserved in salt. Capers should be rinsed (if preserved in salt) and
drained before use. They can be used whole or finely chopped, depending on the recipe.

# 019 Redcurrant & Cranberry Sauce

**PREPARATION TIME** 5 minutes   **COOKING TIME** 25 minutes   **SERVES** 4

115g/4oz/⅓ cup redcurrant jelly
115g/4oz/1 cup cranberries
juice and finely grated zest of 1 orange

1 cinnamon stick
2 tbsp ruby Port

1 Put the redcurrant jelly in a saucepan, add the cranberries, orange juice and zest, cinnamon stick and Port and stir to mix.
2 Bring slowly to the boil, stirring, then simmer, uncovered, for about 20 minutes, or until the cranberries are soft and the sauce thickens slightly, stirring frequently.
3 Serve warm or cold. If serving cold, remove the pan from the heat and set aside until cold. Remove and discard the cinnamon stick before serving.

**SERVING SUGGESTIONS** Serve with grilled or pan-fried lamb cutlets or beef steaks, or with roast venison, pheasant or turkey.
**VARIATION** Use blueberries in place of cranberries.
**COOK'S TIP** Frozen cranberries can also be used for this recipe. If you are using frozen cranberries, they may be used frozen (preferable) or defrosted – you may also need to reduce the overall cooking time a little.

# 020 Cranberry & Orange Sauce

PREPARATION TIME 5 minutes    COOKING TIME 30 minutes    SERVES 6–8

225g/8oz/2 cups cranberries

juice and finely grated zest of 1 small orange

115g/4oz/½ cup caster sugar

1–2 tbsp ruby Port (optional)

1 Put the cranberries in a saucepan with the orange juice, sugar and 150ml/5fl oz/⅔ cup water.

2 Bring slowly to the boil, then cook, uncovered, for 20–30 minutes, or until the cranberries are soft, stirring occasionally.

3 Remove the pan from the heat and let cool slightly. Using a slotted spoon, remove half the cranberries and place in a bowl. Purée the remainder and juice in a blender or food processor.

4 Add the cranberry purée to the reserved cranberries in the bowl, then stir in the orange zest and Port, if using, mixing well. Serve warm or cold.

SERVING SUGGESTIONS Serve with hot or cold roast turkey, chicken, pork or duck.

COOK'S TIP Cranberries are in season and at their peak from late autumn into the winter months. You can also purchase them frozen all year round.

# 021 **Classic Pesto**

**PREPARATION TIME** 10 minutes   **SERVES** 4–6

55g/2oz/2½ cups basil leaves, roughly torn
  into pieces
55g/2oz/½ cup pine nuts
1 garlic clove, crushed

100ml/3½fl oz/⅓ cup extra-virgin olive oil
55g/2oz/heaped ½ cup freshly grated
  Parmesan cheese
salt and freshly ground black pepper

1 Put the basil in a mortar with the pine nuts, garlic and a little of the oil. Pound or grind with a
  pestle to make a paste. Gradually work in the remaining oil, then stir in the Parmesan and
  season to taste with salt and pepper.
2 Alternatively, put the basil, pine nuts, garlic and olive oil in a small blender or food processor
  and blend to form a fairly smooth paste. Add the Parmesan and salt and pepper to taste and
  process briefly to mix.
3 Store the pesto in a screw-topped jar, covered with a thin layer of oil, in the refrigerator for up to
  1 week. Serve cold.

**SERVING SUGGESTIONS** Serve with hot gnocchi or linguine. Alternatively, serve with grilled or roast chicken
portions or haddock cutlets.
**VARIATION** Use 25g/1oz/1¼ cups parsley in place of 25g/1oz/1¼ cups basil.

# 022 Satay Sauce

PREPARATION TIME 10 minutes   COOKING TIME 25 minutes   SERVES 6–8

115g/4oz/scant 1 cup dry roasted or
    unsalted (toasted) peanuts
1 tbsp olive oil
3 shallots, finely chopped
2 garlic cloves, crushed
1 red or green chilli, deseeded and
    finely chopped

2.5cm/1in piece of root ginger, peeled and
    finely chopped
400g/14oz/scant 1⅔ cups tinned coconut
    milk
juice of 1 lime
1 tbsp light soft brown sugar
salt

1 Put the peanuts in a blender or food processor and process until they are finely chopped.
   Set aside.
2 Heat the oil in a saucepan, add the shallots and sauté for about 5 minutes, or until softened.
   Add the garlic, chilli and ginger and sauté for 2 minutes.
3 Remove the pan from the heat, then add the shallot mixture to the peanuts in the processor and
   process briefly to mix.
4 Return the mixture to the saucepan, then stir in the coconut milk, lime juice and sugar.
5 Bring slowly to the boil, stirring, then reduce the heat and simmer, uncovered, for 10–15 minutes,
   or until the sauce is thickened, stirring occasionally. Season with salt, if required. Serve hot.

**SERVING SUGGESTIONS** Serve as a dipping sauce with marinated grilled or barbecued beef or lamb
kebabs. Alternatively, serve with a selection of cooked vegetables or vegetable crudités.

## Chapter 2

# SAUCES FOR PASTA

Pasta comes in a vast array of shapes and sizes and it cries out for the addition of a delicious, home-made sauce. Pasta sauces should be served with freshly cooked hot pasta, either on top of the pasta or tossed lightly together with the pasta. With each recipe in this chapter, a couple of serving suggestions are included, specifying which type of pasta is recommended, but there are no hard and fast rules about this, so use these as a guide only.

A wide selection of tempting pasta sauces are included. Choose from Garlic & Chilli Sauce, Spicy Tomato Sauce, Hazelnut Pesto Sauce, Chorizo & Plum Tomato Sauce, Courgette & Mixed Pepper Sauce, Spinach & Blue Cheese Sauce, Cajun Chicken Sauce or Creamy Smoked Salmon Sauce, as well as old favourites such as Fresh Tomato & Basil Sauce, Bolognese Sauce, Primavera or Classic Carbonara.

Courgette & Mixed Pepper Sauce (see page 39)

# 023 **Primavera Sauce**

**PREPARATION TIME** 15 minutes   **COOKING TIME** 25 minutes   **SERVES** 4

2 carrots, finely diced
2 courgettes, sliced
225g/8oz/2 cups small broccoli florets
115g/4oz asparagus, cut into 2.5cm/1in
   lengths
175g/6oz/1 cup frozen peas
1 bunch spring onions, chopped
1 garlic clove, crushed

400g/14oz/scant 1⅔ cups tinned
   chopped tomatoes
150ml/5fl oz/scant ⅔ cup vegetable stock
   (homemade or from a stock cube)
1 tbsp chopped parsley
1 tbsp chopped basil
salt and freshly ground black pepper

1 Put the carrots, courgettes, broccoli, asparagus, peas, spring onions, garlic, tomatoes, and stock
   in a saucepan, season with salt and pepper in a saucepan and bring slowly to the boil, stirring
   occasionally. Reduce the heat, cover and simmer for 10 minutes, stirring from time to time.
2 Uncover the pan, increase the heat slightly and cook for a further 5–10 minutes, or until the
   vegetables are cooked and tender, stirring occasionally.
3 Stir in the herbs and season again to taste with salt and pepper. Serve hot.

**SERVING SUGGESTIONS** Serve with hot pasta such as fusilli, spirali or riccioli. Sprinkle with freshly grated
Parmesan cheese just before serving, if desired.
**VARIATION** Use sugar-snap peas or frozen baby broad beans in place of peas.

# 024 Garlic & Chilli Sauce

**PREPARATION TIME** 10 minutes   **COOKING TIME** 10 minutes   **SERVES** 4

5 tbsp olive oil

1 small onion, finely chopped

3–4 garlic cloves, finely chopped or crushed

2 small red chillies, finely chopped
  (for a milder flavour, remove and
  discard the seeds)

4 sun-dried tomatoes in oil, drained, patted
  dry and finely chopped

2–3 tbsp chopped parsley or basil

salt and freshly ground black pepper

1 Heat 1 tbsp of the oil in a saucepan, add the onion, garlic and chillies and sauté for about
  5 minutes, or until softened.

2 Add the remaining oil to the pan together with the sun-dried tomatoes. Heat gently until hot,
  stirring continuously.

3 Stir in the herbs and season to taste with salt and pepper. Serve hot.

**SERVING SUGGESTIONS** Serve with hot pasta such as spaghetti, spaghettini or tagliatelle. Sprinkle the
tossed pasta with a generous amount of freshly grated Parmesan cheese just before serving.

**VARIATIONS** Use green chillies in place of red chillies. Use 25–55g/1–2oz/¼–⅓ cup chopped or sliced
pitted black olives in place of sun-dried tomatoes.

# 025 Fresh Tomato & Basil Sauce

PREPARATION TIME 15 minutes    COOKING TIME 35 minutes    SERVES 4

1 tbsp olive oil

6 shallots, finely chopped

2 garlic cloves, finely chopped

2 celery sticks, finely chopped

700g/1lb 9oz tomatoes, skinned, deseeded
  and chopped

4 sun-dried tomatoes in oil, drained, patted
  dry and finely chopped

2 tbsp medium sherry

1 tbsp tomato purée

½ tsp light soft brown sugar

2–3 tbsp chopped basil

salt and freshly ground black pepper

1 Heat the oil in a saucepan, add the shallots, garlic and celery and sauté for about 5 minutes,
  or until softened.

2 Add the tomatoes, sun-dried tomatoes, sherry, tomato purée, sugar, and salt and pepper to
  taste, and mix well. Bring to the boil, then reduce the heat, cover and simmer for 15 minutes,
  stirring occasionally.

3 Uncover the pan, increase the heat slightly and cook for a further 10–15 minutes, or until the
  sauce is cooked and thickened, stirring occasionally. Stir in the basil. Serve hot.

**SERVING SUGGESTIONS** Serve with hot pasta such as penne or fusilli. Sprinkle with freshly grated
Parmesan cheese and garnish with basil sprigs. This sauce is also delicious served with hot filled pasta such
as tortelloni or ravioli.

**VARIATIONS** Use 1–2 leeks in place of shallots. Use 2 small carrots in place of celery. Use chopped mixed
herbs in place of basil.

# 026 **Courgette & Mixed Pepper Sauce**

**PREPARATION TIME** 10 minutes   **COOKING TIME** 30 minutes   **SERVES** 4

55g/2oz butter
1 red onion, finely chopped
1 garlic clove, crushed
1 red pepper, halved, deseeded and diced
1 yellow pepper, halved, deseeded and diced
4 courgettes, sliced
115g/4oz/2 cups button mushrooms, sliced

400g/14oz/scant 1⅔ cups tinned
  chopped tomatoes
150ml/5fl oz/⅔ cup red wine
1 tbsp tomato purée
2 tbsp chopped basil
salt and freshly ground black pepper

1 Melt the butter in a saucepan, add the onion, garlic, red and yellow peppers and courgettes and sauté for about 5 minutes, or until slightly softened. Add the mushrooms, tomatoes, red wine and tomato purée, season to taste with salt and pepper and stir to mix. Bring to the boil, then reduce the heat, cover and simmer for 10 minutes, stirring occasionally.

2 Uncover the pan, increase the heat a little and cook for a further 10–15 minutes, or until the sauce has thickened slightly and the vegetables are tender, stirring occasionally. Stir in the basil and adjust the seasoning to taste. Serve hot.

**SERVING SUGGESTIONS** Serve with hot pasta such as spaghetti or fettuccine.
**VARIATIONS** Use 1 standard onion or 4 shallots in place of red onion. Use dry white wine or vegetable stock in place of red wine.

# 027 **Hazelnut Pesto Sauce**

**PREPARATION TIME** 10 minutes   **SERVES** 4

55g/2oz/2½ cups basil leaves, roughly torn
   into pieces
55g/2oz/½ cup hazelnuts, lightly toasted
2 garlic cloves, crushed

100ml/3½fl oz/⅓ cup olive oil
85g/3oz/½ cup freshly grated
   Parmesan cheese
salt and freshly ground black pepper

1  Put the basil, hazelnuts, garlic and olive oil in a small blender or food processor and blend
   until fairly smooth and thoroughly mixed. Add the Parmesan and salt and pepper to taste and
   process briefly to mix.

2  Alternatively, put the basil in a mortar with the hazelnuts, garlic and a little of the oil. Pound or
   grind with a pestle to make a paste. Gradually work in the remaining oil, then stir in the
   Parmesan and season to taste with salt and pepper.

3  Transfer to a small bowl, cover and set aside in a cool place until ready to serve. Alternatively,
   store the pesto in a screw-topped jar, covered with a thin layer of oil, in the refrigerator for up to
   1 week. Serve cold.

**SERVING SUGGESTIONS** Serve with hot filled pasta such as ravioli. Alternatively, serve with hot pasta such
as plain spaghetti, spinach tagliatelle, farfalle or fusilli.
**VARIATION** Use lightly toasted walnuts or almonds instead of hazelnuts.
**COOK'S TIP** Basil is a delicate-leaved herb that should be prepared carefully. To avoid losing flavour and
colour too quickly, tear the leaves with your fingers instead of chopping with a knife. If you do chop basil with
a knife or scissors, use the chopped leaves as quickly as possible.

# 028 **Spinach & Blue Cheese Sauce**

**PREPARATION TIME** 15 minutes   **COOKING TIME** 15 minutes   **SERVES** 4

25g/1oz butter
4 shallots, finely chopped
1 garlic clove, crushed
25g/1oz/¼ cup plain flour
450ml/16fl oz/1¾ cups milk

350g/12oz spinach, cooked and
  thoroughly drained
115g/4oz Stilton cheese, crumbled
salt and freshly ground black pepper

1 Melt the butter in a saucepan, add the shallots and garlic and sauté for about 5 minutes, or
  until softened. Add the flour and cook for 1 minute, stirring.
2 Remove the pan from the heat and gradually stir or whisk in the milk. Return the pan to the
  heat and cook gently, stirring or whisking continuously, until the sauce comes to the boil and
  thickens. Simmer gently for 2–3 minutes, stirring.
3 Press any excess water out of the spinach using the back of a wooden spoon, then chop the
  spinach. Add the spinach and Stilton to the sauce and mix well.
4 Reheat gently, stirring continuously, until the cheese has melted and the sauce is hot. Season to
  taste with salt and pepper. Serve hot.

**SERVING SUGGESTIONS** Serve with hot pasta such as tagliatelle, linguine or spaghetti.
**VARIATIONS** Use 1 onion in place of shallots. Use diced Gorgonzola, diced Cambozola/blue Brie or grated
mature Cheddar in place of Stilton.
**COOK'S TIP** Other quick and easy ways to squeeze excess water out of the spinach are to tip the cooked
spinach into a colander and press with a potato masher, or press between two plates.

# 029 **Tasty Tuna Sauce**

PREPARATION TIME 10 minutes   COOKING TIME 15 minutes   SERVES 4

55g/2oz butter
225g/8oz leeks (trimmed weight), washed
   and sliced
225g/8oz closed cup mushrooms, sliced
25g/1oz/¼ cup plain flour
425ml/15fl oz/1⅔ cups milk

400g/14oz tinned tuna in spring water,
   brine or oil, drained and flaked
2–3 tbsp chopped parsley
a good pinch cayenne pepper
salt and freshly ground black pepper

1 Melt the butter in a saucepan, add the leeks and mushrooms and sauté gently for about
   10 minutes, or until softened. Add the flour and cook gently for 1 minute, stirring.
2 Remove the pan from the heat and gradually stir or whisk in the milk, then heat gently, stirring
   or whisking continuously, until the sauce comes to the boil and thickens. Simmer gently for
   2–3 minutes, stirring.
3 Stir in the tuna, parsley, cayenne pepper and salt and pepper to taste, then reheat gently until
   hot, stirring. Serve hot.

**SERVING SUGGESTIONS** Serve with hot pasta such as spaghetti, tagliatelle, linguine or spaghettini.
**VARIATIONS** Use flaked canned salmon in place of tuna. Use sliced courgettes in place of mushrooms. Use
1 tbsp chopped tarragon or coriander in place of parsley.

# 030 **Creamy Smoked Salmon Sauce**

PREPARATION TIME 10 minutes   COOKING TIME 15 minutes   SERVES 4

25g/1oz butter
225g/8oz/4 cups button mushrooms, halved
150ml/5fl oz/⅔ cup dry white wine
300ml/10fl oz/1¼ cups crème fraîche

280g/10oz smoked salmon, cut into thin
  strips or small pieces
1 tbsp chopped dill
1 tbsp creamed horseradish sauce
salt and freshly ground black pepper

**1** Melt the butter in a saucepan, add the mushrooms and sauté gently for about 5 minutes,
or until softened.

**2** Add the wine and bring to the boil, then cook over a high heat until the liquid has reduced by
half, stirring occasionally.

**3** Lower the heat, stir in the crème fraîche and simmer.

**4** Stir in the smoked salmon, dill, creamed horseradish sauce and salt and pepper to taste, and
heat gently for 1–2 minutes. Serve hot.

**SERVING SUGGESTIONS** Serve with hot pasta such as linguine, spaghetti, fettuccine or tagliatelle.
**VARIATIONS** Use sliced courgettes in place of mushrooms. Use double cream in place of crème fraîche.
Use chopped flat-leaf parsley or snipped chives in place of dill.
**COOK'S TIP** You can buy smoked salmon trimmings, which are ideal to use in this recipe, and these will be
more economical too.

# 031 **Red Salmon & Watercress Sauce**

**PREPARATION TIME** 10 minutes    **COOKING TIME** 15 minutes    **SERVES** 4

20g/¾oz butter

3 shallots, finely chopped

1 garlic clove, crushed

175g/6oz watercress, washed and
   patted dry

300ml/10fl oz/1¼ cups crème fraîche

1 tsp Dijon mustard

400g/14oz tinned red salmon in brine,
   drained

salt and freshly ground black pepper

1 Melt the butter in a saucepan, add the shallots, garlic and watercress and sauté for about
5 minutes, or until the shallots are softened.

2 Remove the pan from the heat and set aside to cool slightly, then place the watercress mixture
in a blender or food processor. Add the crème fraîche, mustard, and salt and pepper to taste,
and blend until smooth.

3 Transfer the mixture to a saucepan and heat gently until hot, stirring continuously.

4 Flake the salmon, removing any bones, then add the salmon to the sauce. Reheat gently until
hot, stirring continuously. Adjust the seasoning to taste and serve hot.

**SERVING SUGGESTIONS** Serve with hot pasta such as farfalle, conchiglie or penne.
**VARIATIONS** Use 1 small standard onion or red onion in place of shallots. Use flaked tinned pink salmon or
tuna in place of red salmon.

# 032 Cajun Chicken Sauce

**PREPARATION TIME** 15 minutes    **COOKING TIME** 15 minutes    SERVES 4

1 tbsp olive oil
1 onion, finely chopped
1 red pepper, halved, deseeded and sliced
2 small courgettes, cut into matchstick strips
225g/8oz/4 cups button mushrooms, halved
450g/1lb skinless boneless chicken breasts,
    cut into thin strips

1 tbsp Cajun seasoning
1 tbsp cornflour
2 tbsp dry sherry
300ml/10fl oz/1¼ cups chicken stock
    (homemade or from a stock cube)
2 tbsp tomato purée
salt and freshly ground black pepper

1 Heat the oil in a wok or large frying pan, add the onion, red pepper, courgettes and mushrooms
  and stir-fry for 3 minutes.
2 Add the chicken and stir-fry for a further 3–4 minutes, or until the chicken is cooked, then add
  the Cajun seasoning and stir-fry for 1 minute.
3 Blend the cornflour with the sherry until smooth and add to the wok with the stock, tomato
  purée and salt and pepper to taste. Stir-fry until hot and bubbling, then simmer gently for 2–3
  minutes, stirring continuously. Serve hot.

**SERVING SUGGESTIONS** Serve with hot pasta such as tagliatelle, fettuccine or spaghetti.
**VARIATIONS** Use carrots in place of courgettes. Use turkey breast or lean pork in place of chicken.
Use Chinese 5-spice or 7-spice seasoning in place of Cajun seasoning.

# 033 **Chicken, Leek & Mushroom Sauce**

PREPARATION TIME 15 minutes   COOKING TIME 20 minutes   SERVES 4–6

40g/1½oz butter
2 leeks, washed and thinly sliced
225g/8oz/4 cups mushrooms, sliced
40g/1½oz/⅓ cup plain flour
300ml/10fl oz/1¼ cups milk

150ml/5fl oz/⅔ cup chicken stock
   (homemade or from a stock cube), cooled
350g/12oz cooked skinless boneless
   chicken, cut into small pieces
1–2 tbsp chopped parsley
salt and freshly ground black pepper

1 Melt the butter in a saucepan, add the leeks and mushrooms and sauté gently for about
   10 minutes, or until softened.
2 Add the flour and cook for 1 minute, stirring. Remove the pan from the heat and gradually stir
   or whisk in the milk and stock.
3 Return the pan to the heat and cook gently, stirring continuously, until the sauce comes to the
   boil and thickens. Simmer gently for 2–3 minutes, stirring.
4 Add the chicken to the sauce and bring back to the boil, stirring continuously, then simmer
   gently for 5 minutes, stirring occasionally.
5 Stir in the parsley and season to taste with salt and pepper. Serve hot.

SERVING SUGGESTIONS Serve with hot pasta such as fusilli or riccioli.
VARIATIONS Use cooked turkey breast or cooked ham in place of chicken. Use 1 tbsp chopped tarragon,
coriander or mixed herbs in place of parsley.

# 034 Chorizo & Plum Tomato Sauce

PREPARATION TIME 20 minutes   COOKING TIME 30 minutes   SERVES 4

55g/2oz butter

1 red onion, finely chopped

1 small red pepper, halved, deseeded and finely chopped

2 celery sticks, finely chopped

2 garlic cloves, crushed

175g/6oz chorizo sausage, thinly sliced

400g/14oz/scant 1⅔ cups tinned tomatoes

4 sun-dried tomatoes in oil, drained, patted dry and finely chopped

6 tbsp dry white wine

1 tbsp sun-dried tomato purée

2–3 tbsp chopped basil

salt and freshly ground black pepper

1 Melt the butter in a saucepan, add the onion, red pepper, celery and garlic and sauté for 5 minutes. Add the chorizo and sauté for 1 minute.

2 Add the tinned tomatoes, sun-dried tomatoes, white wine, tomato purée, and salt and pepper to taste, and stir to mix, breaking up the tinned tomatoes with the spoon. Bring to the boil, then reduce the heat, cover and simmer for 15 minutes, stirring occasionally.

3 Uncover the pan, increase the heat slightly and cook for a further 5–10 minutes, or until the sauce is cooked and thickened slightly, stirring occasionally. Stir in the basil. Serve hot.

**SERVING SUGGESTIONS** Serve with hot pasta such as tagliatelle or fettuccine.
**VARIATIONS** Use fresh tomatoes in place of tinned tomatoes – skin and chop 500g/1lb 2oz ripe plum or vine-ripened tomatoes and use as directed. Use red wine in place of white wine.

# 035 Carbonara Sauce

**PREPARATION TIME** 10 minutes   **COOKING TIME** 15 minutes   **SERVES** 4

350g/12oz dried spaghetti
25g/1oz butter
1 tbsp olive oil
1 onion, finely chopped
225g/8oz smoked back bacon
   rashers, chopped
3 eggs, beaten

6 tbsp double cream
55g/2oz/⅓ cup freshly grated
   pecorino cheese
85g/3oz/½ cup freshly grated
   Parmesan cheese
2 tbsp chopped parsley or snipped chives
salt and freshly ground black pepper

1 Cook the spaghetti in a large saucepan of lightly salted, boiling water for 10–12 minutes, or until just cooked or al dente.

2 Meanwhile, heat the butter and oil in a saucepan until the butter has melted. Add the onion and sauté for about 5 minutes, or until softened.

3 Add the bacon and cook for about 5 minutes, or until the bacon is cooked, stirring frequently. Remove the pan from the heat and set aside.

4 Mix the eggs, cream, pecorino, two-thirds of the Parmesan, the parsley, and salt and pepper, to taste, together in a bowl.

5 Drain the pasta and return to a clean pan. Add the bacon mixture and toss to mix. Add the egg mixture and cook gently over a very low heat, tossing continuously, until the eggs are just lightly cooked. Sprinkle with the remaining Parmesan and serve immediately.

**SERVING SUGGESTIONS** Serve with other hot pasta, such as tagliatelle, instead of spaghetti.
**VARIATION** Use smoked pancetta, de-rinded, in place of bacon.

# 036 Bolognese Sauce

**PREPARATION TIME** 10 minutes   **COOKING TIME** 1 hour 10 minutes   **SERVES** 4–6

1 tbsp olive oil

2 red onions, chopped

1 carrot, finely chopped

2 celery sticks, finely chopped

1 garlic clove, crushed

500g/1lb 2oz lean minced beef

1 tbsp plain flour

225g/8oz mushrooms/4 cups, sliced

400g/14oz/scant 1⅔ cups tinned tomatoes

1 tbsp tomato purée

300ml/10fl oz/1¼ cups beef or vegetable
    stock (homemade or from a stock cube)

300ml/10fl oz/1¼ cups dry red or
    white wine

2 tsp dried Italian herb seasoning

salt and freshly ground black pepper

1  Heat the oil in a large saucepan, add the onions, carrot, celery and garlic and sauté for about
    5 minutes, or until softened.

2  Add the minced beef and cook until the meat is browned all over, stirring occasionally. Add the
    flour and cook for 1 minute, stirring.

3  Add the mushrooms, tomatoes, tomato purée, stock, wine, dried herb seasoning, and salt and
    pepper to taste, and stir to mix, breaking up the tomatoes with the spoon.

4  Bring to the boil, then reduce the heat, cover and simmer for about 1 hour, stirring occasionally,
    until the meat is cooked and the sauce is well reduced. If desired, uncover the pan and
    increase the heat slightly 15–20 minutes before the end of the cooking time to thicken the
    sauce a little more. Serve hot.

**SERVING SUGGESTIONS** Serve with hot pasta such as spaghetti or spaghettini. Serve sprinkled with freshly
grated Parmesan cheese.

**VARIATIONS** Use lean minced lamb or pork in place of beef. Use extra stock in place of red wine.

# Chapter 3

# SAUCES FOR MEAT & FISH

Freshly grilled or pan-fried meat, poultry or game served with a simple, tasty sauce is a hard combination to beat. In the following pages you'll find a wide variety of appetizing sauces, with something to suit every occasion.

Many of these sauces are relatively quick and easy to make, and will add a delicious finishing touch to a meal. Choose from classics such as Lemon Caper Sauce or Madeira Sauce, or try something a little different such as Plum & Ginger Sauce or Spiced Green Lentil Sauce.

Many types of fish and shellfish are often enhanced when simply grilled, baked or pan-fried, and served with a delicious sauce, such as Marie Rose Sauce, Cheese & Chive Sauce, Dill & Mustard Sauce, Wild Mushroom Sauce, Creamy Fresh Lemon Sauce or Herb & Lime Butter.

Lemon Caper Sauce (see page 65)

# 037 **Wild Mushroom Sauce**

**PREPARATION TIME** 10 minutes   **COOKING TIME** 15 minutes   **SERVES** 4

25g/1oz butter

2 shallots, thinly sliced

1 garlic clove, crushed

350g/12oz mixed wild mushrooms, such as
  shiitake and oyster mushrooms, sliced

2 tbsp dry sherry

2–3 tsp chopped thyme (optional)

2–3 tbsp crème fraîche or soured cream

salt and freshly ground black pepper

1 Melt the butter in a large, non-stick frying pan. Add the shallots and garlic and sauté gently
  for 3 minutes.

2 Add the mushrooms and sauté for about 5 minutes, or until tender.

3 Stir in the sherry and thyme, if using, increase the heat slightly and cook for 2–3 minutes,
  stirring continuously, until most of the liquid has evaporated.

4 Stir in the crème fraîche and season to taste with salt and pepper. Serve hot.

**SERVING SUGGESTIONS** Serve with grilled or pan-fried halibut or salmon steaks, or with grilled or oven-baked whole trout or mackerel.

**VARIATIONS** Use button, chestnut or closed-cup mushrooms (or a mixture) in place of wild mushrooms. Use brandy, ruby Port or Madeira in place of sherry. Use chopped sage or tarragon in place of thyme. Use 1–2 tbsp chopped parsley in place of thyme.

# 038 Dill & Mustard Sauce

**PREPARATION TIME** 5 minutes   **COOKING TIME** 20 minutes   **SERVES** 6

200ml/7fl oz/¾ cup dry white wine
175ml/6fl oz/⅔ cup fish or vegetable stock
   (homemade or from a stock cube)
200ml/7fl oz/¾ cup crème fraîche or
   double cream

2 tbsp wholegrain mustard
2 egg yolks, lightly beaten
2–3 tbsp chopped dill
salt and freshly ground black pepper

1 Put the wine and stock in a saucepan and bring to the boil, then boil rapidly until the liquid has reduced by about half.
2 Reduce the heat and stir in the crème fraîche, mustard, egg yolks and dill.
3 Cook gently, stirring continuously, for about 10 minutes, or until the sauce has thickened slightly. Do not allow the mixture to boil. Season to taste with salt and pepper. Serve hot.

**SERVING SUGGESTIONS** Serve with pan-fried or grilled plaice, lemon sole or halibut fillets, or with pan-fried or barbecued prawns.
**VARIATIONS** Use 1–2 tbsp Dijon mustard in place of wholegrain mustard. Use 1–2 tbsp chopped tarragon or 2–3 tsp horseradish sauce (or to taste) in place of dill.
**COOK'S TIPS** Egg yolks are added to sauces such as this one towards the end of the cooking time. They will enrich and thicken a sauce, but remember that the eggs will curdle if the mixture is boiled.
   Once made, this sauce should be served immediately as it cannot be reheated.

# 039 Sage & Red Onion Sauce

**PREPARATION TIME** 10 minutes   **COOKING TIME** 15 minutes   **SERVES** 4–6

55g/2oz butter
2 red onions, finely chopped
25g/1oz/¼ cup plain flour
150ml/5fl oz/⅔ cup milk
150ml/5fl oz/⅔ cup vegetable stock
   (homemade or from a stock cube), cooled

a squeeze of fresh lime juice
   (optional)
1–2 tbsp chopped sage
salt and freshly ground black pepper

1 Melt half of the butter in a frying pan, add the onions and sauté gently for about
  10 minutes, or until softened. Remove the pan from the heat, set aside and keep hot.
2 Meanwhile, put the remaining butter in a saucepan with the flour, milk, stock and lime juice, if
  using. Heat gently, whisking continuously, until the sauce comes to the boil and thickens.
  Simmer gently for 3–4 minutes, stirring.
3 Stir in the sautéed onions and sage and reheat gently until hot, stirring continuously. Season to
  taste with salt and pepper. Serve hot.

**SERVING SUGGESTIONS** Serve with pan-fried or roast chicken, duck, pheasant or rabbit.
**VARIATION** Use standard onions in place of red onions.

# 040  **Horseradish Butter**

**PREPARATION TIME** 10 minutes, plus chilling  **SERVES** 4–6

115g/4oz unsalted butter
(at room temperature)
1½ tbsp horseradish sauce

2 tbsp finely snipped chives
freshly ground black pepper

1 Put the butter in a small bowl and beat until softened. Add the horseradish sauce, snipped chives and black pepper to taste, and beat until well mixed.

2 Put the flavoured butter onto a piece of cling film and shape into a log. Wrap the butter in the cling film, then chill in the refrigerator for at least 1 hour before serving. Cut into 4–6 even slices to serve. Serve chilled.

**SERVING SUGGESTIONS** Serve a slice of flavoured butter on top of grilled or pan-fried beef, pork or venison steaks, or turkey breast steaks.

# 041 **Chilli Sauce**

**PREPARATION TIME** 10 minutes   **COOKING TIME** 20 minutes   **SERVES** 4–6

400g/14oz/scant 1⅔ cups tinned
  chopped tomatoes
2 shallots, finely chopped
2 celery sticks, finely chopped
1 red chilli, deseeded and finely chopped

1 garlic clove, crushed
150ml/5fl oz/⅔ cup dry white wine
1 tbsp tomato purée
salt and freshly ground black pepper

1 Put the tomatoes, shallots, celery, chilli, garlic, wine, tomato purée, and salt and pepper to taste in a small saucepan and stir to mix.

2 Bring the mixture to the boil, then reduce the heat to medium/low and cook, uncovered, for 15–20 minutes, or until the sauce is cooked and thickened, stirring occasionally. Adjust the seasoning to taste and serve hot.

**SERVING SUGGESTIONS** Serve with stir-fried king prawns tossed with cooked rice noodles. Alternatively, serve with grilled or oven-baked whole sardines or mackerel.
**VARIATIONS** Use red wine or unsweetened apple juice in place of white wine. Use 1–2 tsp hot chilli powder in place of whole chilli. Use 450g/1lb fresh tomatoes, skinned and chopped, in place of tinned tomatoes.

# 042 Spiced Green Lentil Sauce

**PREPARATION TIME** 15 minutes    **COOKING TIME** 1 hour 20 minutes **SERVES** 6–8

1 tbsp olive oil

1 onion, finely chopped

1 carrot, finely chopped

2 celery sticks, finely chopped

1 tsp each ground cumin, ground coriander,
    ground allspice and cayenne pepper

225g/8oz/1 cup green lentils

500ml/18fl oz/2 cups vegetable stock
    (homemade or from a stock cube)

3 tbsp medium sherry

2 tbsp chopped flat-leaf parsley

salt and freshly ground black pepper

1 Heat the oil in a saucepan, add the onion, carrot and celery and sauté gently for about
   10 minutes, or until softened.

2 Stir in the ground spices and cook for 1 minute, stirring. Add the lentils, stock, sherry and salt
   and pepper to taste and mix well.

3 Bring gently to the boil, then cover and simmer for about 1 hour, or until the lentils are cooked
   and soft, stirring occasionally.

4 Stir in the parsley and adjust the seasoning to taste. Serve hot.

**SERVING SUGGESTIONS** Serve with North African-style barbecued lamb or beef and vegetable kebabs.
**COOK'S TIP** If you prefer a smoother sauce, once the lentils are cooked and soft, remove the pan from
the heat and stir in the chopped parsley. Set aside to cool slightly, then purée briefly in a blender or food
processor. Return the sauce to the rinsed-out pan and reheat gently until hot, stirring.

# 043 Cheese & Chive Sauce

**PREPARATION TIME** 5 minutes   **COOKING TIME** 10 minutes   **SERVES** 4

15g/½oz butter
1 tbsp plain flour
150ml/5fl oz/⅔ cup milk
150ml/5fl oz/⅔ cup chicken stock
   (homemade or from a stock cube), cooled

55g/2oz/½ cup grated mature
   Cheddar cheese
2–3 tbsp snipped chives
salt and freshly ground black pepper

1 Put the butter, flour, milk and stock in a saucepan and heat gently, whisking continuously, until
  the sauce comes to the boil and thickens. Simmer gently for 3–4 minutes, stirring.
2 Remove the pan from the heat and stir in the Cheddar until melted. Stir in the snipped chives
  and season to taste with salt and pepper. Serve hot.

**SERVING SUGGESTIONS** Serve with poached smoked haddock fillets, or with pan-fried cod steaks.
**VARIATIONS** Use Gruyère or Emmental cheese in place of Cheddar. Use chopped parsley in place of chives.

# 044 **Marie Rose Sauce**

**PREPARATION TIME** 15 minutes   **SERVES** 4–6

200ml/7fl oz/¾ cup Mayonnaise
   (see page 25)
4 tbsp extra-thick double cream
2 tbsp tomato ketchup
1 tsp Worcestershire sauce

1 tsp fresh lemon or lime juice
2 tsp creamed horseradish sauce (optional)
a few drops of Tabasco sauce
salt and freshly ground black pepper

1 Put the mayonnaise and cream in a bowl and stir until well mixed.

2 Add the tomato ketchup, Worcestershire sauce, lemon juice, creamed horseradish sauce,
   if using, and Tabasco sauce and mix well.

3 Season to taste with salt and pepper. Serve immediately or cover and chill until ready to serve.
   Serve cold.

**SERVING SUGGESTIONS** Serve with cold cooked king prawns, mixed seafood or flaked crab meat.
**COOK'S TIPS** Worcestershire sauce is a strongly flavoured proprietary brown sauce/condiment, which can be
served with roast or grilled meat and poultry, or added to recipes such as this one, or to salad dressings or
other sauces to heighten the flavour.
   Fiery Tabasco sauce also adds flavour and heat to some sauces, marinades and salad dressings.

# 045 **Creamy Curry Sauce**

PREPARATION TIME 10 minutes   COOKING TIME 20 minutes   SERVES 4–6

40g/1½oz butter
1 onion, finely chopped
1 garlic clove, crushed
2 tbsp plain flour
3 tbsp medium-hot curry paste

1 tbsp tomato purée
250ml/9fl oz/1 cup vegetable or chicken
    stock (homemade or from a stock cube)
200ml/7fl oz/¾ cup single cream
salt and freshly ground black pepper

1 Melt the butter in a saucepan, add the onion and sauté gently for 8–10 minutes.

2 Add the garlic and sauté for 1 minute, then add the flour and cook for 1 minute, stirring.
Stir in the curry paste and tomato purée. Remove the pan from the heat and gradually stir
or whisk in the stock.

3 Return the pan to the heat and heat gently, stirring or whisking continuously, until the sauce
comes to the boil and thickens. Simmer gently for 2–3 minutes, stirring.

4 Stir in the cream and reheat gently until hot but not boiling, stirring continuously. Season to
taste with salt and pepper. Serve hot.

**SERVING SUGGESTIONS** Serve with grilled or pan-fried pork or lamb chops, or chicken thighs.

# 046 **Madeira Sauce**

**PREPARATION TIME** 5 minutes   **COOKING TIME** 10 minutes   **SERVES** 4

1 tbsp olive oil

6 shallots, sliced

4 tbsp vegetable stock (homemade or
  from a stock cube)

4 tbsp Madeira

1 tsp dried herbes de Provence

2 tbsp crème fraîche

salt and freshly ground black pepper

1 Heat the oil in a saucepan, add the shallots and sauté for 5 minutes, or until softened.

2 Stir in the stock, Madeira and dried herbs, then bring the mixture to the boil and simmer,
  uncovered, for 2 minutes, stirring occasionally.

3 Stir in the crème fraîche and heat gently until hot, stirring continuously. Season to taste with salt
  and pepper. Serve hot.

**SERVING SUGGESTIONS** Serve with pan-fried lamb's liver or kidneys, or chicken livers.
**VARIATIONS** Use 1 onion in place of shallots. Use ruby Port or red wine in place of Madeira.

# 047 **Red Wine Gravy**

PREPARATION TIME 10 minutes   COOKING TIME 25 minutes   SERVES 4–6

25g/1oz butter, softened

2 tbsp plain flour

1 small onion, roughly chopped

300ml/10fl oz/1¼ cups beef or lamb stock
  (homemade or from a stock cube)

100ml/3½fl oz/⅓ cup full-bodied red wine

pan juices from roast meat (such as beef,
  lamb or pork)

salt and freshly ground black pepper

**1** Put half of the butter and all the flour in a small bowl and mix together until well blended to make a beurre manié. Set aside.

**2** Melt the remaining butter in a small saucepan, add the onion and sauté gently for about 10 minutes, or until softened.

**3** Stir the stock, wine and the juices from the roast meat into the onions and bring to the boil. Reduce the heat, cover and simmer for 5 minutes.

**4** Remove the onion from the pan using a fine slotted spoon and discard (or strain the mixture through a sieve and return the liquid to the pan).

**5** Bring the liquid back to the boil, then add the beurre manié a little at a time, whisking continuously to blend in well with the liquid, until all the beurre manié has been added. Continue to cook, whisking, until the gravy thickens.

**6** Simmer gently for 5 minutes, stirring continuously. Season to taste with salt, if required, and black pepper. Serve hot.

**SERVING SUGGESTIONS** Serve with roast beef, lamb or pork.
**VARIATION** To make a chicken gravy, use chicken stock and white wine in place of beef or lamb stock and red wine.

# 048 White Wine & Mussel Sauce

**PREPARATION TIME** 10 minutes   **COOKING TIME** 10 minutes   **SERVES** 4

2 tbsp cornflour
350ml/12fl oz/1⅓ cups dry or
  medium white wine
200g/7oz cooked shelled mussels
  (shelled weight)

15g/½oz butter
3 tbsp crème fraîche
2 tbsp chopped flat-leaf parsley
salt and freshly ground black pepper

1 Put the cornflour and a little of the wine and blend until smooth. Stir in the remaining wine,
  then heat gently, stirring continuously, until the sauce comes to the boil and thickens. Simmer
  gently for 3 minutes, stirring.
2 Stir in the mussels, butter, crème fraîche, parsley and salt and pepper to taste and heat gently
  until hot, stirring continuously. Serve hot.

**SERVING SUGGESTIONS** Serve with grilled or barbecued tuna or salmon steaks.
**COOK'S TIP** To clean mussels, scrub them in a sinkful of cold water, scraping off barnacles and pulling away
the beards. Discard any mussels with broken shells or open mussels that don't close when tapped sharply.
Once cooked, discard any mussels that remain closed.

# 049 **Lemon Caper Sauce**

PREPARATION TIME 5 minutes   COOKING TIME 10 minutes   SERVES 4

25g/1oz butter

25g/1oz/¼ cup plain flour

300ml/10fl oz/1¼ cups milk

2 tbsp drained capers (chopped, if desired)

1 tbsp vinegar from jar of capers

finely grated zest of 1 small lemon

salt and freshly ground black pepper

1 Put the butter, flour and milk in a saucepan and heat gently, whisking continuously, until the sauce comes to the boil and is thickened and smooth. Simmer gently for 3–4 minutes, stirring.

2 Stir in the capers, vinegar and lemon zest and reheat gently until almost boiling. Season to taste with salt and pepper. Serve hot.

**SERVING SUGGESTIONS** Serve with char-grilled turkey breast, pork or lamb steaks.
**VARIATIONS** Use half milk and half vegetable stock in place of milk. Use white wine vinegar or fresh lemon juice in place of caper vinegar.

# 050 **Herb & Lime Butter**

**PREPARATION TIME** 10 minutes, plus chilling    **SERVES** 4–6

115g/4oz unsalted butter
  (at room temperature)
finely grated zest of 1 lime

2 tbsp chopped parsley
1 tbsp chopped coriander
freshly ground black pepper

1 Put the butter in a small bowl and beat until softened. Add the lime zest, parsley, coriander, and black pepper to taste, and beat until well mixed.

2 Put the flavoured butter onto a piece of cling film and shape into a log. Wrap the butter in the cling film, then chill in the refrigerator for at least 1 hour before serving. Cut into 4–6 even slices to serve. Serve chilled.

**SERVING SUGGESTION** Serve a slice of flavoured butter on top of cooked hot fresh mussels.
**VARIATIONS** Use the finely grated zest of 1 lemon or 1 small orange in place of lime zest. Use chopped tarragon, oregano or basil in place of coriander.

# 051 **Creamy Fresh Lemon Sauce**

**PREPARATION TIME** 5 minutes   **COOKING TIME** 15 minutes   **SERVES** 4

1 tbsp sunflower oil
2 onions, thinly sliced
2 garlic cloves, crushed
1 red or green chilli, deseeded and
   finely chopped

juice and finely grated zest of 2 lemons
150ml/5fl oz/⅔ cup crème fraîche
salt and freshly ground black pepper

1 Heat the oil in a saucepan, add the onions, garlic and chilli and sauté for 5 minutes.
2 Add the lemon juice and zest, then cover and cook gently for about 10 minutes, or until the
   onions are soft, stirring occasionally.
3 Add the crème fraîche and reheat gently until hot, stirring. Season to taste with salt and pepper.
   Serve hot.

**SERVING SUGGESTIONS** Serve with grilled haddock, cod or halibut steaks.

# 052 Plum & Ginger Sauce

**PREPARATION TIME** 20 minutes   **COOKING TIME** 20 minutes   **SERVES** 6

1 tbsp sunflower oil

1 small red onion, finely chopped

1 garlic clove, crushed

2 tsp (peeled) grated fresh
　root ginger

350g/12oz red dessert plums, halved,
　pitted and chopped

150ml/5fl oz/²⁄₃ cup red wine

25g/1oz light soft brown sugar

1 tbsp brandy or sherry (optional)

1 Heat the oil in a saucepan, add the onion, garlic and ginger and sauté for 5 minutes. Add the plums and sauté for 1 minute, stirring.

2 Stir in the wine and sugar and heat gently, stirring continuously, until the sugar has dissolved. Bring slowly to the boil, then reduce the heat, cover and simmer for about 10 minutes, or until the plums are soft.

3 Remove the pan from the heat and let cool slightly, then purée the mixture in a blender or food processor until smooth.

4 Return the sauce to the rinsed-out pan and stir in the brandy, if using. Reheat gently until hot, stirring continuously. Serve hot or cold.

5 If serving the sauce cold, remove the pan from the heat and allow the sauce to cool completely before serving.

**SERVING SUGGESTIONS** Serve with crispy duck and spring onions in Chinese pancakes. Alternatively, serve with grilled beef, pork or lamb.

# Chapter 4

# SALSAS, RELISHES & SALAD DRESSINGS

Salsas and relishes not only add that wonderful finishing touch to many meals, they also add delicious texture, flavour and colour to grilled, pan-fried or oven-baked meat, poultry, fish and shellfish. Choose from a wide variety of flavourful recipes, including Salsa Verde, Red Onion Salsa, Mango Salsa, Red Hot Relish and Chunky Corn Relish.

Salad dressings, vinaigrettes and mayonnaises are really what make a salad, bringing together all its separate ingredients to create a delicious combination of flavours. Enjoy such classics as French Dressing, Tomato & Basil Dressing, Sweet & Sour Dressing, Raspberry Vinaigrette, Garlic & Herb Mayonnaise and Moroccan-Spiced Mayonnaise. Alternatively, try a warm dressing, such as Hot Chilli Dressing.

Red Onion Salsa (see page 73)

# 053 Salsa Verde

**PREPARATION TIME** 10 minutes, plus standing   **SERVES** 4

1 small onion, finely chopped
2 garlic cloves, crushed
4 tbsp chopped parsley
2 tbsp chopped mint
1 tbsp snipped chives
1 tbsp capers, drained and chopped

4 tbsp extra-virgin olive oil
2 tbsp freshly squeezed lemon or lime juice
1 tsp Dijon mustard
a few drops of Tabasco sauce, or to taste
salt and freshly ground black pepper

1 Put the onion, garlic, herbs and capers in a small bowl and stir to mix. Add the olive oil, lemon juice and mustard and mix well. Stir in the Tabasco sauce and salt and pepper to taste.

2 Cover and leave to stand at room temperature for about 30 minutes before serving, to allow the flavours to develop.

**SERVING SUGGESTIONS** Serve with grilled lamb, pork or beef steaks. Alternatively, serve with grilled monkfish or rainbow trout and roasted mixed vegetables.
**VARIATION** Omit the Tabasco sauce and add 1 deseeded and finely chopped red or green chilli.
**COOK'S TIP** If you prefer a smoother salsa, simply process all the ingredients together in a small blender or food processor until thoroughly combined.

# 054 **Red Onion Salsa**

**PREPARATION TIME** 15 minutes, plus standing  **SERVES** 4

3 ripe tomatoes

2 tbsp tomato juice or passata

1 tbsp olive oil

1 red onion, finely chopped

2 tsp horseradish sauce

1 tbsp chopped parsley

salt and freshly ground black pepper

**1** Using a sharp knife, cut a small cross in the base of each tomato. Put the tomatoes in a heatproof bowl, cover them with boiling water and leave for about 30 seconds, or until the skins split.

**2** Using a slotted spoon, remove the tomatoes from the bowl and plunge into cold water, then drain well.

**3** Peel off and discard the skins, then halve the tomatoes and discard the seeds. Finely chop the flesh and put it in a bowl.

**4** Add the tomato juice, olive oil, onion, horseradish sauce and parsley to the tomato flesh and stir to mix well. Season to taste with salt and pepper.

**5** Cover and leave to stand at room temperature for about 1 hour before serving, to allow the flavours to develop.

**SERVING SUGGESTIONS** Serve with grilled good-quality pork or lamb sausages. Alternatively, serve with grilled or barbecued salmon or tuna steaks, or with grilled or pan-fried field (portobello) mushrooms.
**VARIATIONS** Use plum or vine-ripened tomatoes in place of standard tomatoes. Use a standard onion in place of red onion. Add ½ deseeded red pepper, finely chopped, with the onion.
**COOK'S TIP** For extra heat and flavour, use hot horseradish sauce.

# 055 **Spiced (Black-Eyed) Bean Salsa**

**PREPARATION TIME** 20 minutes, plus standing    **SERVES** 4–6

1 tbsp olive oil

1 tbsp clear honey

juice and finely grated zest of 1 lemon

2 tsp hot chilli sauce, or to taste

400g/14oz tinned black-eyed beans, rinsed and drained

1 small red onion, finely chopped

½ small yellow pepper, halved, deseeded and finely chopped

1 red chilli, deseeded and finely chopped

1 garlic clove, crushed

2 tbsp chopped coriander

salt and freshly ground black pepper

1 Put the olive oil, honey, lemon juice and zest and hot chilli sauce in a bowl and whisk together until thoroughly mixed.

2 Add the beans, onion, yellow pepper, chilli, garlic and coriander and toss to mix well. Season to taste with salt and pepper.

3 Cover and leave to stand at room temperature for about 1 hour before serving, to allow the flavours to develop.

**SERVING SUGGESTIONS** Serve with grilled or barbecued king prawns or char-grilled salmon steaks.

# 056 **Chunky Corn Relish**

**PREPARATION TIME** 10 minutes, plus standing  **SERVES** 4–6

4 spring onions, finely chopped

8 red radishes, finely chopped

1 small red pepper, halved, deseeded and finely chopped

200g/7oz tinned sweetcorn kernels, drained

1 tbsp olive oil

2 tsp freshly squeezed lemon juice

1 tsp Dijon mustard

2–3 tbsp snipped chives

salt and freshly ground black pepper

**1** Put the spring onions, radishes and red pepper in a bowl. Add the sweetcorn kernels and stir to mix well.

**2** In a separate bowl, whisk together the olive oil, lemon juice, mustard, chives, and salt and pepper to taste. Pour the mustard mixture over the sweetcorn and toss to mix well.

**3** Cover and leave to stand at room temperature for about 30 minutes before serving, to allow the flavours to develop.

**SERVING SUGGESTIONS** Serve with grilled home-made beef burgers. Alternatively, serve with grilled or barbecued beef, pork or chicken kebabs or good-quality beef or pork sausages.
**VARIATIONS** Use 2–3 shallots or 1 small red onion in place of spring onions. Use chopped flat-leaf parsley or 1–2 tbsp chopped mixed herbs in place of chives.

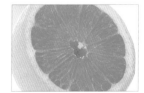

# 057 **Mango Salsa**

**PREPARATION TIME** 10 minutes, plus standing   **SERVES** 4

1 large ripe mango, peeled, pitted and
   finely chopped
55g/2oz cucumber, finely chopped

2–3 spring onions, finely chopped
1–2 tbsp chopped coriander
salt and freshly ground black pepper

1 Put the mango, cucumber, spring onions and coriander in a bowl and stir to mix thoroughly.
  Season to taste with salt and pepper.

2 Cover and leave to stand at room temperature for about 30 minutes before serving, to allow the
  flavours to develop.

**SERVING SUGGESTIONS** Serve with grilled or barbecued chicken drumsticks. Alternatively, serve with char-
grilled salmon or tuna steaks.
**VARIATION** Use 1 small pineapple in place of mango.
**COOK'S TIPS** When buying mangoes, choose sweet-smelling fruits with tight, smooth, unblemished skins
that give slightly when pressed gently.
  For this recipe, the cucumber can be peeled, if preferred. However, leaving the peel on the cucumber will
add extra texture and colour to this salsa.

# 058 Pineapple & Ginger Salsa

**PREPARATION TIME** 25 minutes, plus standing   **SERVES** 4

350g/12oz prepared fresh pineapple,
   finely chopped
2 tsp (peeled) finely chopped fresh
   root ginger

1 tbsp clear honey
1 tsp freshly squeezed lime juice
2 tbsp chopped coriander
freshly ground black pepper

1 Put the pineapple and ginger in a bowl and stir to mix. Add the honey and lime juice and toss
   to mix. Stir in the coriander and season to taste with black pepper.
2 Cover and leave to stand at room temperature for about 30 minutes before serving, to allow the
   flavours to develop. Drain off any excess juices before serving, if desired.

**SERVING SUGGESTIONS** Serve with char-grilled chicken or duck breasts, or salmon or tuna steaks.
**VARIATION** Use prepared fresh mango in place of pineapple.

# 059 **Char-Grilled Pepper Relish**

**PREPARATION TIME** 20 minutes, plus cooling and standing   **COOKING TIME** 15 minutes   **SERVES** 4

2 yellow peppers

½ small red onion, finely chopped

1 red chilli, deseeded and finely chopped

4 tsp olive oil

2 tbsp chopped coriander

2 tsp medium chilli sauce, or to taste

salt and freshly ground black pepper

1 Preheat the grill to high. Cut the peppers in half lengthways and put them, cut-side down, on the rack in a grill pan.

2 Cook the peppers under the hot grill for 10–15 minutes, or until the skins are blackened and charred. Remove the grill pan from the heat, cover the peppers with a clean, damp tea towel and leave to cool.

3 Once they are cool, remove the skin, core and seeds from the peppers, then finely chop the flesh and put it in a bowl.

4 Add the onion, chilli, olive oil and coriander to the pepper flesh and mix well. Stir in the chilli sauce, and salt and pepper to taste, mixing well.

5 Cover and leave to stand at room temperature for about 1 hour before serving, to allow the flavours to develop.

**SERVING SUGGESTIONS** Serve with barbecued beef, pork or turkey steaks or kebabs, or with cold cooked sliced meats such as beef, ham or pork. Alternatively, serve with grilled goat's cheese.
**VARIATIONS** Use 2 red peppers or 1 yellow and 1 red pepper in place of yellow peppers. Use 1 green chilli in place of red chilli.

# 060 **Red Hot Relish**

PREPARATION TIME 15 minutes, plus standing   SERVES 4

450g/1lb plum or vine-ripened tomatoes,
  skinned, deseeded and finely chopped
2 shallots, finely chopped
1 red or green chilli, deseeded and
  finely chopped
1 garlic clove, crushed

2 sun-dried tomatoes in oil, drained, patted
  dry and finely chopped
1 tbsp olive oil
1 tbsp chopped oregano or marjoram
a few drops of Tabasco sauce (optional)
salt and freshly ground black pepper

1 Put the plum tomatoes, shallots, chilli, garlic and sun-dried tomatoes in a bowl and stir well.
2 Add the olive oil, oregano and Tabasco, if using, and mix well. Season to taste with salt
  and pepper.
3 Cover and leave to stand at room temperature for about 1 hour before serving, to allow the
  flavours to develop.

SERVING SUGGESTIONS Serve with grilled or oven-baked tuna or salmon steaks, or chicken wings.

# 061 **French Dressing**

**PREPARATION TIME** 10 minutes   **SERVES** 4–6

6 tbsp extra-virgin olive oil

2 tbsp white wine vinegar or cider vinegar
or lemon juice

1–2 tsp Dijon mustard, to taste

a pinch caster sugar

1 small garlic clove, crushed

1–2 tbsp chopped mixed herbs

salt and freshly ground black pepper

1 Put all the ingredients in a small bowl and whisk together until thoroughly mixed.

2 Alternatively, put all the ingredients in a clean screw-top jar, seal and shake well until thoroughly mixed.

3 Adjust the seasoning to taste and serve immediately, or keep in a screw-top jar in the refrigerator for up to 1 week. Whisk or shake thoroughly before serving.

**SERVING SUGGESTION** Serve with a baby leaf or mixed green salad.

# 062 Hot Chilli Dressing

**PREPARATION TIME** 10 minutes   **COOKING TIME** 5 minutes   **SERVES** 6

4 tbsp olive oil

2 shallots, finely chopped

1 red chilli, deseeded and finely chopped

6 tbsp passata

2 tbsp red wine vinegar

1 tsp Dijon mustard

salt and freshly ground black pepper

1 Heat 1 tbsp of the oil in a saucepan, add the shallots and chilli and sauté for about 5 minutes, or until softened. Remove the pan from the heat.

2 Put the sautéed shallots and chilli in a small blender or food processor with the remaining oil, the passata, vinegar, mustard, and salt and pepper to taste and blend until smooth and well mixed.

3 Adjust the seasoning to taste and serve immediately, or keep in a screw-top jar in the refrigerator for up to 3 days. Whisk or shake thoroughly before serving.

4 Alternatively, serve the dressing warm, if desired. Simply return the blended mixture to the pan and reheat gently until warm, stirring continuously, then serve.

**SERVING SUGGESTIONS** Serve with chickpea or broad bean falafel and lettuce in pitta bread, or with a mixed bean or pasta salad.

**VARIATIONS** Use 1 small red onion in place of shallots. Use tomato juice in place of passata.

**COOK'S TIP** Use ½–1 tsp ready-prepared chopped red chillies, or to taste, in place of preparing your own red chilli.

# 063  Coriander & Lime Dressing

**PREPARATION TIME** 10 minutes   **SERVES** 8–10

150ml/5fl oz/⅔ cup unsweetened white
grape juice

6 tbsp white wine vinegar

4 tbsp sunflower oil or light olive oil

2 tbsp chopped coriander

finely grated zest of 1 lime

juice of 2 limes

1 tsp caster sugar

salt and freshly ground black pepper

1 Put the grape juice, vinegar, oil, coriander, lime zest, lime juice, sugar, and salt and pepper to taste in a small bowl and whisk together until thoroughly mixed.

2 Alternatively, put all the ingredients in a clean screw-top jar, seal and shake well until thoroughly mixed.

3 Adjust the seasoning to taste and serve immediately, or keep in a screw-top jar in the refrigerator for up to 3 days. Whisk or shake thoroughly before serving.

**SERVING SUGGESTIONS** Serve with a salad of char-grilled or pan-fried halloumi cheese and mixed green leaves. Alternatively, serve with a cold cooked chicken, pork or duck salad.

**VARIATIONS** Use lemon zest and juice in place of lime zest and juice. Use chopped mixed herbs in place of coriander.

# 064 Tomato & Basil Dressing

**PREPARATION TIME** 10 minutes  **SERVES** 4

5 tbsp passata

1 tbsp extra-virgin olive oil

2 tsp balsamic vinegar

a pinch caster sugar

2 tbsp chopped basil

salt and freshly ground black pepper

1 Put the passata, oil, vinegar, sugar, basil and salt and peppter to taste in a small bowl and whisk together until thoroughly mixed.

2 Alternatively, put all the ingredients in a clean screw-top jar, seal and shake well until thoroughly mixed.

3 Adjust the seasoning to taste and serve immediately, or keep in a screw-top jar in the refrigerator for up to 3 days. Whisk or shake thoroughly before serving.

**SERVING SUGGESTIONS** Serve with a mixed Mediterranean-style vegetable salad. Alternatively, serve with a pasta or mixed bean salad.

# 065 Sweet & Sour Dressing

**PREPARATION TIME** 10 minutes   **SERVES** 6–8

3 tbsp olive oil

3 tbsp unsweetened apple juice

2 tbsp red wine vinegar

2 tbsp clear honey

2 tbsp light soy sauce

2 tbsp tomato ketchup

2 tbsp medium sherry

1 garlic clove, crushed

1 tsp ground ginger

salt and freshly ground black pepper

1 Put all the ingredients in a small bowl and whisk together until thoroughly mixed.

2 Alternatively, put all the ingredients in a clean screw-top jar, seal and shake well until thoroughly mixed.

3 Adjust the seasoning to taste and serve immediately, or keep in a screw-top jar in the refrigerator for up to 3 days. Whisk or shake thoroughly before serving.

**SERVING SUGGESTIONS** Serve with a mixed bean or noodle salad, or with a warm stir-fried chicken or mixed seafood salad.

# 066 **Walnut & Parsley Vinaigrette**

PREPARATION TIME 10 minutes   SERVES 8–10

4 tbsp walnut oil
3 tbsp red wine vinegar
3 tbsp cider vinegar
150ml/5fl oz/²⁄₃ cup unsweetened
   red grape juice

1 garlic clove, crushed
1 tsp French or Dijon mustard
a good pinch caster sugar
2 tbsp chopped parsley
salt and freshly ground black pepper

1 Put the oil, red wine and cider vinegars, grape juice, garlic, mustard, sugar and parsley in a small bowl and whisk together until thoroughly mixed. Season to taste with salt and pepper.
2 Alternatively, put all the ingredients in a clean screw-top jar, seal and shake well until thoroughly mixed.
3 Adjust the seasoning to taste and serve immediately, or keep in a screw-top jar in the refrigerator for up to 3 days. Whisk or shake thoroughly before serving.

**SERVING SUGGESTIONS** Serve with a mixed bean or garden salad, or with cooked hot vegetables such as green beans, asparagus or artichokes.

# 067 **Raspberry Vinaigrette**

**PREPARATION TIME** 10 minutes   **SERVES** 12–14

400g/14oz/scant 1⅔ cups tinned
  raspberries in fruit juice
125ml/4fl oz/½ cup red wine vinegar
5 tbsp sunflower oil or light olive oil

1 tsp caster sugar
1 tsp dried sage
salt and freshly ground black pepper

1 Put the raspberries and their juice in a blender or food processor and blend until smooth. Push the raspberry purée through a nylon sieve into a bowl and discard the pips and pulp.
2 Put the raspberry purée, vinegar, oil, sugar, sage and salt and pepper to taste in a small bowl and whisk together until thoroughly mixed.
3 Alternatively, put all the ingredients in a clean screw-top jar, seal and shake well until thoroughly mixed.
4 Adjust the seasoning to taste and serve immediately, or keep in a screw-top jar in the refrigerator for up to 3 days. Whisk or shake thoroughly before serving.

**SERVING SUGGESTIONS** Serve with strips of char-grilled vegetables such as courgettes or aubergines, sprinkled with toasted chopped walnuts, if desired. Alternatively, serve with a mixed bean or rice salad, or mixed salad leaves.
**VARIATIONS** Use dried oregano, marjoram or thyme in place of sage. Use white wine or cider vinegar in place of red wine vinegar.

# 068 Orange Vinaigrette

**PREPARATION TIME** 10 minutes   **SERVES** 8–10

150ml/5fl oz/⅔ cup unsweetened
   orange juice
3 tbsp cider vinegar
3 tbsp white wine vinegar

3 tbsp extra-virgin olive oil
1 tsp finely chopped rosemary
½ tsp caster sugar
salt and freshly ground black pepper

1 Put all the ingredients in a small bowl and whisk together until thoroughly mixed.
2 Alternatively, put all the ingredients in a clean screw-top jar, seal and shake well until
   thoroughly mixed.
3 Adjust the seasoning to taste and serve immediately, or keep in a screw-top jar in the
   refrigerator for up to 3 days. Whisk or shake thoroughly before serving.

**SERVING SUGGESTIONS** Serve with a carrot, cracked wheat, couscous or mixed dark leaf salad.
**VARIATION** Use freshly squeezed orange juice, if preferred.

# 069 Moroccan-Spiced Mayonnaise

**PREPARATION TIME** 20 minutes    **COOKING TIME** 2 minutes    **SERVES** 6

3 tbsp tomato juice

½ tsp each ground cumin, ground coriander, paprika, turmeric, cinnamon and ground ginger

1 garlic clove, crushed (optional)

6 tbsp Mayonnaise (see page 25)

4 tbsp natural yogurt

2–3 tbsp chopped coriander

salt and freshly ground black pepper

1 Put the tomato juice, ground spices and garlic, if using, in a small saucepan and cook gently for 2 minutes, stirring continuously. Remove the pan from the heat and set aside to cool.

2 Put the mayonnaise, yogurt, spice mixture and chopped coriander in a small bowl and stir to mix thoroughly. Season to taste with salt and pepper.

3 Serve immediately, or cover and leave to stand in a cool place for about 30 minutes before serving. Store in a covered container in the refrigerator for up to 1 day. Serve cold.

**SERVING SUGGESTIONS** Serve with cold cooked new potatoes, or with a mixed bean, rice or pasta salad.
**VARIATION** Increase the ground spices to 1 tsp each for a more pronounced spicy flavour.

# 070 Garlic & Herb Mayonnaise

PREPARATION TIME 10 minutes   SERVES 6–8

1 recipe quantity Mayonnaise
  (see page 25)
1 garlic clove, crushed

2 tbsp chopped mixed herbs, such as
  parsley, chives, basil and oregano
salt and freshly ground black pepper

1 Make the mayonnaise according to the instructions given, adding the crushed garlic with the
  egg yolks.
2 Fold the mixed herbs into the garlic mayonnaise just before serving. Season to taste with salt
  and pepper.
3 Serve immediately, or cover and chill until required. Store in a covered container in the
  refrigerator for up to 2 days. Serve cold.

**SERVING SUGGESTIONS** Serve with oven-roasted or char-grilled mixed Mediterranean vegetables.
Alternatively, serve with cold cooked sliced pork, ham, salami or smoked turkey, or smoked mackerel fillets.
**COOK'S TIP** Garlic is available all year round because it can be dried and stored successfully. A neatly plaited
bunch of garlic will keep well for several months in a dry, airy place.

# Chapter 5

# LIGHT SAUCES & SAVOURY & SWEET DIPS

Everyone loves a delicious sauce as an accompaniment to a meal, but some sauces are not so good for the waistline. This chapter enables you to enjoy some lighter, healthier versions of classic sauces, such as Light Béchamel Sauce, Light Thousand Island Sauce and Light Burgundy Sauce.

A great way to entertain family and friends at a party is to serve a tempting selection of flavourful home-made dips, such as Red Pepper Hummus, Creamy Garlic & Chive Dip and Watercress Cheese Dip, with fresh vegetable crudités, warm pitta bread fingers, breadsticks or tortilla chips for dipping. For sweet dips, such as Honey Yogurt Dip, Lemon Cream Swirl and Wicked Chocolate Fondue, serve with a selection of prepared fresh fruit, small squares of fudge, marshmallows or fingers of chocolate brownies.

Spicy Roast Aubergine Dip (see page 105)

# 071 **Light Béchamel Sauce**

**PREPARATION TIME** 35 minutes, plus standing   **COOKING TIME** 10 minutes   **SERVES** 4

1 small onion or 2 shallots, sliced

1 small carrot, sliced

½ celery stick, roughly chopped

1 bay leaf

6 black peppercorns

several parsley stalks

300ml/10fl oz/1¼ cups semi-skimmed milk

25g/1oz reduced-fat spread

25g/1oz/¼ cup plain flour

salt and freshly ground black pepper

1 Put the onion, carrot, celery, bay leaf, peppercorns and parsley in a saucepan with the milk and bring slowly to the boil. Remove the pan from the heat and set aside to infuse for 30 minutes.

2 Strain the mixture into a jug, reserving the milk and discarding the contents of the sieve. Melt the reduced-fat spread in a small saucepan over a low heat, then stir in the flour and cook gently for 1 minute, stirring.

3 Remove from the heat and gradually whisk in the flavoured milk. Return the pan to the heat and bring slowly to the boil, whisking continuously, until the sauce is thickened and smooth. Simmer gently for 2–3 minutes, stirring. Season to taste with salt and pepper. Serve hot.

**SERVING SUGGESTIONS** Serve with char-grilled skinless chicken or turkey breast, grilled cod or haddock fillets, braised celery or baby broad beans.
**VARIATIONS** Just before serving, stir in 55g/2oz/½ cup grated reduced-fat mature Cheddar or 2–3 tbsp chopped parsley.

# 072 **Light Tarragon Sauce**

**PREPARATION TIME** 5 minutes   **COOKING TIME** 10 minutes   **SERVES** 6

25g/1oz reduced-fat spread
25g/1oz/¼ cup plain flour
300ml/10fl oz/1¼ cups vegetable or
    chicken stock (homemade or from a
    stock cube), cooled
150ml/5fl oz/⅔ cup semi-skimmed milk

1 tbsp tarragon vinegar
1 tbsp chopped tarragon
2 tsp French or Dijon mustard
55g/2oz/½ cup finely grated reduced-fat
    mature Cheddar cheese
salt and freshly ground black pepper

1 Put the reduced-fat spread, flour, stock and milk in a small saucepan. Heat gently, whisking continuously, until the sauce comes to the boil and is thickened and smooth. Simmer gently for 3–4 minutes, stirring.

2 Stir in the vinegar, tarragon and mustard and reheat gently until hot, stirring.

3 Remove the pan from the heat and stir in the Cheddar until melted. Season to taste with salt and pepper. Serve hot.

**SERVING SUGGESTION** Serve with char-grilled or oven-baked skinless chicken breasts.

# 073 **Quick Tomato Sauce**

**PREPARATION TIME** 10 minutes   **COOKING TIME** 25 minutes   **SERVES** 6

40g/1½oz reduced-fat spread
1 onion, finely chopped
400g/14oz/scant 1⅔ cups tinned
   chopped tomatoes

1 tbsp tomato purée
1 tsp dried herbes de Provence
4 tbsp dry white wine
salt and freshly ground black pepper

1 Melt the reduced-fat spread in a saucepan over a low heat. Add the onion and cook gently for
   5 minutes, stirring occasionally.
2 Add the tomatoes, tomato purée, dried herbs, and salt and pepper to taste, and mix well.
3 Bring almost to the boil, stir in the wine, then bring to the boil, reduce the heat and simmer,
   uncovered, for 15–20 minutes, or until the sauce is cooked and thickened, stirring occasionally.
   Serve hot.

**SERVING SUGGESTIONS** Serve with char-grilled or barbecued tuna or salmon steaks. Alternatively, serve
with poached or oven-baked cod or haddock fillets, skinless chicken breasts or grilled polenta slices.
**VARIATIONS** Add 1 crushed garlic clove to the tomato sauce, if desired. Cook the garlic with the onion and
continue as above. Use 1 red onion or 4 shallots in place of standard onion. Use 1 tbsp chopped mixed
herbs in place of dried herbs.
**COOK'S TIP** If you prefer a smoother sauce, remove the pan from the heat and allow the cooked sauce
to cool slightly, then purée the sauce in a blender or food processor until smooth. Return the sauce to the
rinsed-out pan and reheat gently before serving.

# 074 **Light Green Peppercorn Sauce**

**PREPARATION TIME** 5 minutes   **COOKING TIME** 10 minutes   **SERVES** 4–6

15g/½oz reduced-fat spread

2 tbsp plain flour

150ml/5fl oz/⅔ cup vegetable stock
  (homemade or from a stock cube), cooled

150ml/5fl oz/⅔ cup semi-skimmed milk

1 tbsp green peppercorns in brine, drained
  and chopped or crushed

25g/1oz/¼ cup smoked hard cheese,
  finely grated

salt and freshly ground black pepper

1 Put the reduced-fat spread, flour, stock and milk in a small saucepan. Heat gently, whisking continuously, until the sauce comes to the boil and is thickened and smooth. Simmer gently for 3–4 minutes, stirring.

2 Remove the pan from the heat and stir in the peppercorns, then stir in the cheese until melted. Season to taste with salt and pepper. Serve hot.

**SERVING SUGGESTIONS** Serve with grilled skinless chicken or turkey breast. Alternatively, serve with poached salmon, cod or haddock steaks.

**VARIATIONS** Use extra milk in place of stock. Use mature Cheddar, Emmental or Gruyère cheese in place of smoked cheese.

**COOK'S TIP** Black, white and green peppercorns all come from the fruit of the same tropical Asian vine, but are picked at different stages and processed differently, which affects their flavour. Black peppercorns have the strongest flavour, followed by white peppercorns, then green.

# 075 **Light Thousand Island Sauce**

**PREPARATION TIME** 10 minutes, plus standing   **SERVES** 8–10

300ml/10fl oz/1¼ cups reduced-calorie
mayonnaise
4 tbsp natural yogurt
2 tbsp tomato ketchup
55g/2oz/3 tbsp drained and
finely chopped gherkins

2 tbsp deseeded and finely chopped
red pepper
2 tbsp deseeded and finely chopped
green or yellow pepper
1 tbsp chopped parsley or coriander
salt and freshly ground black pepper

1 Put the mayonnaise, yogurt and tomato ketchup in a bowl and stir to mix. Add the gherkins,
peppers and parsley and mix well. Season to taste with salt and pepper.

2 Cover and leave in a cool place for about 30 minutes before serving, to allow the flavours to
develop. Serve cold.

**SERVING SUGGESTIONS** Serve with cold cooked prawns or a cold cooked mixed seafood salad.
**VARIATIONS** Use chopped pitted stuffed or green olives in place of green or yellow pepper. Add 1–2 cold
hard-boiled eggs, shelled and mashed or finely chopped, to the sauce, if desired.

# 076 **Light Espagnole Sauce**

**PREPARATION TIME** 15 minutes   **COOKING TIME** 1¼ hours   **SERVES** 4–6

25g/1oz reduced-fat spread

1 lean back bacon rasher, finely chopped

2 shallots, finely chopped

1 small carrot, finely chopped

55g/2oz/1 cup chestnut or brown-cap
   mushrooms, finely chopped

3 tbsp plain flour

550ml/19fl oz/2¼ cups beef stock
   (homemade or from a stock cube)

1 dried bouquet garni

4 black peppercorns

1 bay leaf

2 tbsp tomato purée

salt and freshly ground black pepper

1 Melt the reduced-fat spread in a saucepan over a low heat, then add the bacon and cook for 2 minutes, stirring. Add the shallots, carrot and mushrooms and cook gently for 8–10 minutes, or until lightly browned, stirring occasionally.

2 Stir in the flour and cook gently until lightly browned, stirring continuously, then remove the pan from the heat and gradually stir in the stock.

3 Add the bouquet garni, peppercorns, bay leaf, tomato purée, and salt and pepper to taste, then return the pan to the heat and bring slowly to the boil, stirring continuously, until the mixture thickens. Cover and simmer gently for 1 hour, stirring the sauce occasionally.

4 Strain the sauce through a sieve into a bowl, remove and discard the bouquet garni, then push the pulp through the sieve. Return the sauce to the rinsed-out pan and discard the contents of the sieve. Reheat the sauce gently until hot, stirring, then adjust the seasoning to taste. Serve hot.

**SERVING SUGGESTIONS** Serve with grilled or roast lean beef, lamb, venison or pheasant.

# 077 **Light Burgundy Sauce**

**PREPARATION TIME** 10 minutes  **COOKING TIME** 15 minutes  **SERVES** 6

25g/1oz reduced-fat spread
1 small red onion, coarsely grated
1 garlic clove, crushed
25g/1oz/¼ cup plain flour
200ml/7fl oz/¾ cup burgundy or red wine

250ml/9fl oz/1 cup beef stock (homemade
  or from a stock cube)
2 tsp chopped thyme
1 tbsp freshly squeezed lemon juice
salt and freshly ground black pepper

1 Melt the reduced-fat spread in a saucepan over a low heat. Add the onion and garlic and cook gently for about 5 minutes, or until softened, stirring occasionally.
2 Stir in the flour and cook for 1 minute, stirring, then remove the pan from the heat and gradually stir in the wine and stock. Return the pan to the heat and bring slowly to the boil, stirring or whisking continuously, until the sauce thickens. Simmer gently for 2–3 minutes, stirring.
3 Stir in the thyme and lemon juice and season to taste with salt and pepper. Serve hot.

**SERVING SUGGESTIONS** Serve with grilled or roast lean beef, lamb, pork, pheasant or low-fat sausages.
**VARIATIONS** Use 2 shallots in place of onion. For a white wine sauce, use chicken or fish stock and medium white wine in place of beef stock and red wine, and serve it with grilled chicken breasts.

# 078 Minted Apple Sauce

**PREPARATION TIME** 10 minutes   **COOKING TIME** 15 minutes   **SERVES** 4–6

1 small onion, finely chopped
450g/1lb cooking apples, peeled, cored
    and sliced

small bunch mint leaves, finely chopped
2 tbsp caster sugar or light soft brown sugar,
    or to taste

1 Put the onion and apples in a saucepan with 2 tbsp water. Cover and cook gently for about
   10 minutes, or until the apples and onion are softened, stirring occasionally.
2 Remove the pan from the heat and mash the apples and onion lightly to form a pulp.
3 Stir in the mint and sugar, then reheat gently, stirring continuously, until the sugar has
   dissolved. Taste, and add a little more sugar, if desired. Serve hot or cold. If serving cold,
   remove the pan from the heat and set aside to cool completely, then serve.

**SERVING SUGGESTIONS** Serve with hot or cold roast or grilled lean gammon or smoked pork.

# 079 **Red Pepper Hummus**

**PREPARATION TIME** 10 minutes   **SERVES** 8–10

420g/15oz tinned chickpeas, rinsed
  and drained
115g/4oz roasted red peppers in oil (drained
  weight), drained and patted dry
1 large garlic clove, crushed
1 tbsp freshly squeezed lemon juice

4 tbsp extra-virgin olive oil, plus extra
  (optional) for drizzling
2 tbsp light tahini
½ tsp hot chilli powder, or to taste
salt and freshly ground black pepper

1 Put the chickpeas, red peppers and garlic in a small blender or food processor and blend to mix.
2 Add the lemon juice, olive oil, tahini, chilli powder, and salt and pepper to taste and blend until
  smooth and well mixed. Adjust the seasoning to taste.
3 Transfer the mixture to a bowl and drizzle with a little extra oil, if desired. Serve.

**SERVING SUGGESTIONS** Serve with breadsticks or vegetable crudités such as courgette and celery sticks,
spring onions and baby sweetcorn.

# 080 **Creamy Garlic & Chive Dip**

**PREPARATION TIME** 5 minutes    **SERVES** 6

150ml/5fl oz/²⁄₃ cup soured cream
150ml/5fl oz/²⁄₃ cup plain fromage frais
2 garlic cloves, crushed
2 shallots, finely chopped (optional)

2–3 tbsp snipped chives, plus extra
   (optional) to serve
salt and freshly ground black pepper

1 Put the soured cream and fromage frais in a bowl and mix until well blended.
2 Add the garlic, shallots, if using, and snipped chives and mix well. Season to taste with salt and pepper.
3 Transfer the mixture to a serving bowl and serve immediately, or cover and chill until ready to serve. Sprinkle with snipped chives, if desired, just before serving.

**SERVING SUGGESTIONS** Serve with grilled or pan-fried goujons of breaded white fish or chicken. Alternatively, serve with oven-baked potato wedges.
**VARIATIONS** Use crème fraîche or natural Greek yogurt in place of soured cream. Use ½ small red onion or 2 spring onions in place of shallots. Use other chopped herbs such as parsley or mixed herbs in place of chives.
**COOK'S TIP** Chive flowers create an attractive garnish for this dip.

# 081 **Watercress Cheese Dip**

PREPARATION TIME 10 minutes, plus chilling   SERVES 6–8

225g/8oz/1 cup full-fat soft cheese
3 tbsp crème fraîche
70g/2½oz watercress, finely chopped

1 garlic clove, crushed
salt and freshly ground black pepper

1 Put the soft cheese in a bowl and stir until softened a little more. Stir in the crème fraîche until well combined.

2 Stir in the watercress and garlic, then season to taste with salt and pepper.

3 Cover and chill for at least 1 hour before serving, to allow the flavours to develop.

SERVING SUGGESTIONS Serve with breadsticks, crackers or a selection of vegetable crudités.

# 082 **Spicy Roast Aubergine Dip**

**PREPARATION TIME** 20 minutes, plus cooling  **COOKING TIME** 30–45 minutes  **SERVES** 6

2 aubergines, cut into chunks or
  large dice
1 onion, sliced
2 garlic cloves, thinly sliced
150ml/5fl oz/²⁄₃ cup tomato juice

1 tsp each hot chilli powder, ground
  coriander and ground cumin
2 tbsp olive oil
juice of 1 lemon
salt and freshly ground black pepper

**1** Preheat the oven to 200°C/400°F/gas mark 6. Put all the ingredients in a non-stick roasting tin and toss together to mix well. Cover with foil and bake in the oven for 30–45 minutes, or until the vegetables are cooked and tender, stirring once or twice.

**2** Remove from the oven and set aside to cool, leaving the foil on.

**3** Once cool, purée the mixture in a blender or food processor until smooth and well mixed. Adjust the seasoning to taste, transfer the mixture to a bowl, cover and chill until ready to serve.

**SERVING SUGGESTIONS** Serve with a selection of warm Middle-Eastern flatbreads cut into fingers or triangles, and vegetable crudités such as carrot and pepper sticks.
**VARIATIONS** Use 1 red chilli, deseeded and finely chopped, in place of chilli powder. Use 2 leeks, trimmed and washed, in place of onion. Use lime or orange juice in place of lemon juice.

# 083 **Creamy Crab Dip**

**PREPARATION TIME** 20 minutes   **SERVES** 8–10

225g/8oz/1 cup full-fat soft cheese
2 tbsp Mayonnaise (see page 25)
2 tsp freshly squeezed lemon juice
½ small red pepper, deseeded and
   finely chopped
2 spring onions, finely chopped

1 garlic clove, crushed
225g/8oz tinned white crab meat (drained
   weight), drained and flaked
2 tbsp chopped parsley
salt and freshly ground black pepper

1 Put the soft cheese in a small bowl and beat until softened a little more. Stir in the mayonnaise
   and lemon juice until smooth.
2 Add the red pepper, spring onions and garlic and mix well. Add the crab meat and parsley and
   stir to mix. Season to taste with salt and pepper.
3 Serve immediately, or cover and chill for 1 hour before serving.

**SERVING SUGGESTIONS** Serve with breadsticks, small crackers or a selection of vegetable crudités such as
celery and carrot sticks, baby sweetcorn and broccoli florets.

# 084 Honey Yogurt Dip

**PREPARATION TIME** 5 minutes   **SERVES** 6–8

225ml/8fl oz/¾ cup natural Greek yogurt
115ml/4fl oz/½ cup thick natural bio yogurt

2 tbsp clear honey, or to taste
½ tsp cinnamon

1 Put the Greek and bio yogurts in a bowl and fold gently together.

2 Fold in the honey and cinnamon, mixing gently until well combined. Serve immediately.

**SERVING SUGGESTIONS** Serve with prepared fruit such as apple and pear wedges, peach or nectarine slices, chunks of banana (brushed with lemon juice to prevent discolouration) and whole strawberries and raspberries or loganberries.

**VARIATIONS** Use maple syrup or golden syrup in place of honey. Use ground mixed spice or ginger in place of cinnamon.

**COOK'S TIP** Use clear, runny honey rather than thick honey for this recipe, as it is easier to combine with other ingredients such as yogurt.

# 085 **Wicked Chocolate Fondue**

**PREPARATION TIME** 5 minutes   **COOKING TIME** 10 minutes   **SERVES** 4

225g/8oz good-quality plain chocolate,
  broken into squares
55g/2oz butter, diced

150ml/5fl oz/²⁄₃ cup double cream
2 tbsp golden syrup
2 tbsp brandy (optional)

1 Put the chocolate, butter, cream and golden syrup in a heatproof serving bowl. Put the bowl over a pan of simmering water and heat until the ingredients are melted, well blended and smooth, stirring occasionally. Stir in the brandy, if using, mixing well.

2 Put the bowl of hot chocolate fondue on a heatproof mat on the table. Alternatively, pour the chocolate fondue into a fondue pan and set the pan over the fondue burner (on a very low heat) at the table. Serve immediately.

**SERVING SUGGESTIONS** Dip prepared fresh fruit such as whole strawberries, cherries, pineapple chunks and apricot halves in the chocolate fondue, using either forks or your fingers. Other foods suitable for dipping include dried fruit, whole nuts, marshmallows, sponge fingers and small pieces of sponge cake.

# 086 **Lemon Cream Swirl**

PREPARATION TIME 10 minutes  SERVES 8–10

225ml/8fl oz/¾ cup double cream
175ml/6fl oz/⅔ cup plain fromage frais

finely grated zest of 1 lemon
5 tbsp luxury lemon curd

1 Put the cream and fromage frais in a bowl and whip together until the mixture thickens and
  holds its shape. Fold in the lemon zest.

2 Transfer the cream mixture to a serving bowl, then spoon the lemon curd over the top.

3 Lightly fold the lemon curd into the whipped cream mixture using a metal spoon to create
  a swirly, marbled effect. Serve immediately.

**SERVING SUGGESTIONS** Serve with a selection of prepared mixed berries such as strawberries, raspberries
and blueberries, and lemon shortcake biscuits or shortbread fingers.

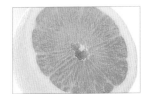

## Chapter 6

# SWEET SAUCES & COULIS

Many desserts are just not the same without the addition of an accompanying sauce to tempt your tastebuds. Sweet sauces and fruit coulis often add that special finishing touch to a dessert, providing an extra treat at mealtimes.

In this chapter there is a wide selection of delicious sweet sauces, all of which are sure to impress your family and friends. Choose from old favourites such as Butterscotch Sauce, Rich Chocolate Sauce and Rum & Raisin Sauce, or enjoy delectable delights such as Yummy Chocolate Fudge Sauce, Creamy Orange Sauce and Orange Marmalade Sauce. Also included are a colourful collection of flavourful fruit coulis, such as Raspberry Vodka Coulis, Golden Nectarine Coulis and Blackcurrant Coulis.

Summer Strawberry Sauce (see page 119)

# 087 Yummy Chocolate Fudge Sauce

**PREPARATION TIME** 5 minutes   **COOKING TIME** 10 minutes   **SERVES** 4–6

115g/4oz/⅔ cup packed light soft
  brown sugar
115g/4oz/½ cup caster sugar
55g/2oz butter, diced

55g/2oz good-quality plain chocolate,
  broken into squares
3 tbsp golden syrup
a few drops of vanilla extract
4 tbsp single cream

1 Put the sugars, butter, chocolate and syrup in a small, heavy-based saucepan. Heat gently until the mixture is well blended and smooth, stirring continuously. Bring to the boil and simmer very gently for 5 minutes, stirring.

2 Remove the pan from the heat, add the vanilla extract and cream and mix thoroughly. Serve hot.

**SERVING SUGGESTIONS** Serve with vanilla or other flavoured ice cream, or with profiteroles or sliced fruit such as pears, peaches or bananas.

**VARIATIONS** Use good-quality milk chocolate in place of plain chocolate. Use canned evaporated milk in place of cream.

**COOK'S TIPS** Choose a good-quality, plain, dark chocolate for this recipe, ideally one containing a high percentage of cocoa solids, often labelled as 'Continental' chocolate.

When storing soft brown sugar, keep it moist by storing in an airtight container with one or two wedges of apple, or a piece of fresh bread.

# 088 **Rich Chocolate Sauce**

**PREPARATION TIME** 5 minutes   **COOKING TIME** 10 minutes   **SERVES** 4–6

175g/6oz good-quality plain chocolate,
  broken into squares
100ml/3½fl oz/⅓ cup double cream
55g/2oz/¼ cup packed light or dark soft
  brown sugar

55g/2oz/¼ cup golden syrup
15g/½oz butter

1 Put the chocolate, cream, sugar, golden syrup and butter in a small, heavy-based saucepan.
  Heat gently, stirring continuously, until the chocolate has melted and the sugar has dissolved.
2 Bring slowly to the boil, stirring continuously, until the mixture is blended and smooth, then
  simmer very gently for 1–2 minutes, stirring occasionally. Let cool slightly before serving, then
  serve hot.

**SERVING SUGGESTIONS** Serve with chocolate profiteroles or scoops of vanilla ice cream.

# 089 **Butterscotch Sauce**

**PREPARATION TIME** 5 minutes   **COOKING TIME** 10 minutes   **SERVES** 6

175g/6oz/scant 1 cup packed light soft
  brown sugar
150ml/5fl oz/⅔ cup double cream

55g/2oz butter, diced
115g/4oz/⅓ cup golden syrup
a few drops of vanilla extract

1 Put the sugar, cream, butter and golden syrup in a small, heavy-based saucepan.
2 Bring slowly to the boil, stirring occasionally, until the sauce is well blended and smooth.
3 Just as the sauce reaches a gentle boil, remove the pan from the heat and stir in the
  vanilla extract.
4 Serve hot or cold (at room temperature, not chilled). If serving the sauce cold, stir it well
  before serving.

**SERVING SUGGESTIONS** Serve with raw or baked sliced bananas, or with baked sponge puddings or
scoops of vanilla or butterscotch ice cream.
**VARIATIONS** Use dark soft brown sugar in place of light soft brown sugar. Use maple syrup in place of
golden syrup.
**COOK'S TIP** If soft brown sugar becomes hard during storage, place the sugar in a microwave-proof dish and
add a wedge of apple. Cover and microwave on HIGH for 30 seconds. Remove and discard the apple, and
stir the sugar well – it should now be softened.

# 090 Rich Mocha Sauce

**PREPARATION TIME** 5 minutes   **COOKING TIME** 15 minutes   **SERVES** 4–6

4 tsp custard powder

1 tbsp light soft brown sugar or caster sugar

300ml/10fl oz/1¼ cups full-fat milk

1–2 tsp instant coffee granules, or to taste

55g/2oz plain chocolate, roughly chopped

a few drops of vanilla extract (optional)

1 Put the custard powder and sugar in a small bowl. Add a little of the milk and blend together to form a smooth paste, then set aside.

2 In a separate small heatproof bowl, dissolve the coffee granules in 1 tbsp boiling water. Add the dissolved coffee to the custard paste and stir to mix well. Set aside.

3 Put the remaining milk in a small, heavy-based saucepan, add the chocolate and heat gently until the chocolate has melted and the mixture is almost boiling, stirring occasionally.

4 Gradually pour the hot chocolate milk onto the blended custard mixture, stirring continuously, until smooth.

5 Return the mixture to the pan and heat gently, stirring continuously, until the custard sauce comes to the boil and thickens. Simmer gently for 1–2 minutes, stirring.

6 Stir in the vanilla extract, if using. Serve hot.

**SERVING SUGGESTIONS** Serve with steamed or baked sponge puddings, or upside-down fruit puddings, or with poached, baked or grilled fruit such as pears or peaches.

**COOK'S TIP** Choose full-fat milk for this recipe, to achieve a delicious, creamy flavour. Semi-skimmed milk can be used as an alternative, to create a slightly less rich sauce, if preferred.

# 091 **Creamy Orange Sauce**

**PREPARATION TIME** 10 minutes  **SERVES** 6–8

150ml/5fl oz/²⁄₃ cup double cream

150ml/5fl oz/²⁄₃ cup plain fromage frais

4 tbsp luxury orange curd

finely grated zest of 1 small orange (optional)

1 Put the cream and fromage frais in a bowl and whip together until the mixture thickens and holds its shape in soft peaks.

2 Gently fold in the orange curd and orange zest, if using, until well combined. Serve cold.

**SERVING SUGGESTIONS** Serve with raspberry tartlets or poached figs, or with fruit such as raspberries, sliced strawberries or mixed summer berries.

**VARIATIONS** Use the finely grated zest of 1 lemon in place of orange zest. Use luxury lemon curd in place of luxury orange curd. Fold the orange curd and orange zest into 300ml/10fl oz/1¼ cups crème fraîche in place of whipped cream and fromage frais, if desired. Use 150ml/5fl oz/²⁄₃ cup extra thick double cream in place of fromage frais for a richer sauce, if desired.

**COOK'S TIPS** Before whipping the cream and fromage frais together, chill the whisk and bowl as well as the cream, to achieve maximum whipped volume. Use a balloon or spiral hand whisk or an electric whisk, but be careful not to over-whip the mixture.

# 092 **Rum & Raisin Sauce**

**PREPARATION TIME** 5 minutes   **COOKING TIME** 10 minutes   **SERVES** 4–6

1 tbsp cornflour
200ml/7fl oz/¾ cup milk
100ml/3½fl oz/⅓ cup double cream
15g/½oz butter

1 tbsp light soft brown sugar, or to taste
2 tbsp rum
55g/2oz/⅓ cup raisins, roughly chopped

1 Put the cornflour and 2 tbsp of the milk in a small bowl and blend until smooth. Set aside.
2 Heat the remaining milk, the cream and butter in a small, heavy-based saucepan until almost boiling. Gradually pour the hot milk and cream mixture onto the cornflour mixture, stirring continuously.
3 Return the mixture to the saucepan and bring slowly to the boil, stirring continuously, until the sauce is thickened and smooth. Simmer gently for 2–3 minutes, stirring.
4 Stir in the sugar, rum and raisins and reheat gently until hot, stirring. Serve hot.

**SERVING SUGGESTIONS** Serve with hot pancakes or crêpes and ice cream, or with mince pies.
**VARIATIONS** Use chopped sultanas, dried cherries or ready-to-eat dried figs or apricots in place of raisins.
Use brandy or whisky in place of rum.

# 093 Summer Strawberry Sauce

**PREPARATION TIME** 10 minutes   **COOKING TIME** 15 minutes   **SERVES** 6

225g/8oz/2 cups ripe strawberries
juice and finely grated zest of 2 lemons

55g/2oz/¼ cup caster sugar, or to taste
1 tsp arrowroot

1 Put the strawberries in a blender or food processor and blend until smooth.
2 Pour the strawberry purée into a saucepan and stir in 150ml/5fl oz/²⁄₃ cup water, the lemon
  juice and zest and sugar.
3 Heat gently, stirring continuously, until the sugar has dissolved, then bring the mixture to the
  boil and simmer gently for 5 minutes, stirring occasionally.
4 Put the arrowroot and 1 tbsp cold water in a small bowl and blend until smooth. Gradually stir
  the arrowroot mixture into the hot strawberry purée and mix well.
5 Reheat gently, stirring continuously, until the sauce comes to the boil and thickens slightly.
  Serve hot.

**SERVING SUGGESTIONS** Serve with chilled lemon or vanilla cheesecake, fruit kebabs, fruit jelly, sorbet or
scoops of ice cream or frozen yogurt.
**VARIATION** Use 1 orange in place of 2 lemons.
**COOK'S TIP** Add an extra ½ –1 tsp arrowroot, if you prefer a slightly thicker sauce.

# 094 **Blueberry Syrup**

PREPARATION TIME 5 minutes plus standing   COOKING TIME 10–15 minutes   SERVES 6–8

225g/8oz/heaped 1 cup caster sugar
225g/8oz/2 cups blueberries

juice of 1 lemon

1 Put the sugar and 150ml/5fl oz/⅔ cup water in a small, heavy-based saucepan and heat gently until the sugar has dissolved, stirring continuously.
2 Add the blueberries, then bring slowly to the boil, stirring continuously. Simmer gently for 3–5 minutes, stirring.
3 Stir in the lemon juice, then remove the pan from the heat and set aside for 5 minutes. Serve warm.

**SERVING SUGGESTIONS** Serve with steamed plain or fruit sponge puddings, hot pancakes or crêpes.

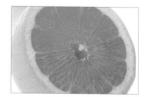

# 095 Orange Marmalade Sauce

**PREPARATION TIME** 5 minutes   **COOKING TIME** 10 minutes   **SERVES** 4

juice of 1 orange
5 tbsp orange marmalade
2 tsp arrowroot

1–2 tsp brandy or whisky, or to taste
(optional)

1 Pour the orange juice into a measuring jug and make up to 150ml/5fl oz/⅔ cup with cold
  water. Pour the diluted orange juice into a small saucepan, add the marmalade and stir to mix.
2 Heat gently, stirring continuously, until the marmalade has dissolved, then bring the mixture
  slowly to the boil, stirring occasionally.
3 Put the arrowroot and 1 tbsp cold water and blend until smooth, then stir the arrowroot mixture
  into the marmalade sauce.
4 Reheat gently, stirring continuously, until the sauce comes to the boil and thickens.
5 Stir in the brandy or whisky, if using. Serve hot.

**SERVING SUGGESTIONS** Serve with individual steamed or baked sponge puddings, or with fruit pies or
puddings, scoops of vanilla, chocolate or other flavoured ice cream, or grilled fruit such as mango, bananas
or nectarines.
**VARIATIONS** Use lemon and lime marmalade in place of orange marmalade and omit the brandy, if desired.
Use orange-flavoured liqueur in place of brandy or whisky.
**COOK'S TIP** Use shredless, fine-cut/shred or thick-cut/shred orange marmalade for this recipe.

# 096 **Melba Sauce**

**PREPARATION TIME** 10 minutes   **COOKING TIME** 5 minutes   **SERVES** 4

4 tbsp redcurrant or blackcurrant jelly
225g/8oz/2 cups raspberries
25g/1oz/¼ cup icing sugar, sifted

1 tbsp framboise (raspberry liqueur) or
   Kirsch (cherry liqueur), or to taste

1 Put the redcurrant jelly in a small saucepan and heat gently until melted, stirring continuously.
   Remove the pan from the heat and set aside.
2 Put the raspberries in a small blender or food processor. Add the melted jelly, sugar and liqueur
   and blend to a smooth purée.
3 Press the fruit purée through a nylon sieve into a bowl, then discard the contents of the sieve.
   Pour the raspberry sauce into a jug and serve cold.

**SERVING SUGGESTIONS** Serve with poached fruit such as peaches, nectarines or pears, or with fruit-filled
meringues or a pavlova.
**VARIATIONS** Use seedless raspberry jam in place of redcurrant or blackcurrant jelly. Use blackberries,
loganberries or mixed berries in place of raspberries.

# 097 **Kiwi & Lime Sauce**

**PREPARATION TIME** 10 minutes plus standing   **SERVES** 8–10

8 ripe kiwi fruit (about 450g/1lb total
    weight), peeled and quartered
juice and finely grated zest of 1 lime
115g/4oz/½ cup medium-fat or full-fat
    soft cheese

150ml/5fl oz/⅔ cup single cream
55g/2oz/¼ cup icing sugar, sifted,
    or to taste

1 Put the kiwi fruit and lime juice and zest in a blender or food processor and blend until smooth.

2 Add the soft cheese and cream and blend until thoroughly mixed.

3 Pour the sauce into a bowl. Stir the icing sugar into the sauce until well combined.

4 Cover and leave the sauce to stand in a cool place for about 30 minutes before serving, to allow
    the flavours to develop. Stir well before serving. Serve cold.

**SERVING SUGGESTIONS** Serve with fruit kebabs, fruit salad or fruit compote.
**VARIATIONS** Use 1 small lemon in place of lime. Use crème fraîche, plain fromage frais or natural Greek
yogurt in place of single cream.
**COOK'S TIPS** Use ripe kiwi fruit for this sauce, to achieve the best flavour. Kiwi fruit are ripe and ready to eat
if they yield slightly when lightly pressed.

# 098 **Blackcurrant Coulis**

**PREPARATION TIME** 15 minutes, plus cooling and chilling   **COOKING TIME** 15 minutes   **SERVES** 4–6

350g/12oz/3 cups blackcurrants, topped
   and tailed
85g/3oz/½ cup packed light soft brown
   sugar, or to taste

1–2 tbsp crème de cassis (blackcurrant
   liqueur), or to taste

**1** Put the blackcurrants in a saucepan with the sugar and 2 tbsp cold water and heat gently, stirring continuously, until the sugar has dissolved. Bring slowly to the boil, then cover and cook gently for about 10 minutes, or until the blackcurrants are soft and pulpy, stirring occasionally.

**2** Remove the pan from the heat, let cool slightly, then press the blackcurrant pulp and juices through a nylon sieve into a bowl. Discard the contents of the sieve.

**3** Stir the crème de cassis into the blackcurrant purée, then taste for sweetness and stir in a little extra sugar and liqueur, if necessary.

**4** Set aside to cool, then cover and chill before serving. Serve cold. The coulis may also be served hot, if preferred.

**SERVING SUGGESTIONS** Serve with French apple tart, hot pancakes or crêpes, meringues, scoops of ice cream, frozen yogurt or sorbet, or with prepared fruit such as figs or peaches.

# 099 **Raspberry Vodka Coulis**

**PREPARATION TIME** 10 minutes   **SERVES** 4

225g/8oz/2 cups raspberries
15g/½oz/1 tbsp icing sugar, sifted,
   or to taste

dash or two of iced vodka, or to taste

1 Put the raspberries in a small blender or food processor and blend to form a purée. Press the raspberry purée through a nylon sieve into a bowl to remove the seeds. Discard the contents of the sieve.

2 Add the icing sugar to the raspberry purée to taste, stirring or whisking to mix well. Stir in the iced vodka to taste. Serve cold.

**SERVING SUGGESTIONS** Serve with mixed berries or strawberries, or with summer pudding.

# 100 **Golden Nectarine Coulis**

**PREPARATION TIME** 20 minutes   **COOKING TIME** 15–20 minutes   **SERVES** 6

4 ripe nectarines, peeled, halved and pitted

2 tbsp freshly squeezed orange juice

2 tbsp caster sugar, or to taste

2–3 tsp orange-flavoured liqueur or brandy, or to taste (optional)

1 Roughly chop the nectarine flesh, then put in a saucepan with the orange juice and sugar. Heat gently, stirring continuously, until the sugar has dissolved. Bring slowly to the boil, then cover and simmer for 10–15 minutes, or until the fruit is soft, stirring occasionally.

2 Remove pan from the heat and let cool slightly. Mash the fruit mixture, or purée it in a blender or food processor, then press it through a nylon sieve into a bowl. Discard the contents of the sieve.

3 Stir the liqueur or brandy, if using, into the purée and taste for sweetness. Add a little extra sugar, if necessary. Serve hot or cold.

**SERVING SUGGESTIONS** Serve with mixed fruit sorbets or ice cream.

# INDEX